JÁN LACIKA
THE LOW TATRAS

COMPILED BY: DANIEL KOLLÁR

The Low Tatras (Nízke Tatry)
1st edition, 2001

Editors: Peter Augustini and Daniel Kollár
Hiking tours: Ján Lacika
Natural settings: Ján Lacika
Natural landmarks and points of interests: Daniel Kollár
Responsible editor: Daniel Kollár
Technical editor: Tibor Kollár
Translation: HACON
Photographs: Karol Demuth, Ladislav Janiga, Miroslav Vážny
Attitude profiles: Ján Lacika
Cartography: © Vojenský kartografický ústav, š. p., Harmanec, 2001
Cover: Ján Hladík
Design and layout: Jagus DTP
Print: Kníhtlačiareň Svornosť, a.s., Bratislava

This guidebook is also available in the Slovak, English, German and Polish languages. Any, including partial, use of this work is permitted only with the written consent of GEOINFO Slovakia Foundation and DAJAMA publishers. The publisher is not liable to legal responsibility for the way of use of this guidebook.

© GEOINFO Slovakia, Ľubľanská 2, 831 02 Bratislava
© DAJAMA, Klimkovičova 1, 841 01 Bratislava

ISBN 80-88975-32-8

Dear readers,

The purpose of the DAJAMA publishers since the beginning of its existence is to promote the regions of Slovakia publishing guidebooks to its geographical and historical assets. Within the series Regions without frontiers the individual boundary areas were presented and the series Visiting Slovakia introduced the potential reader to the history and present of the natural historic regions. All books are prepared not only in the Slovak language but also in several foreign languages. Precisely the translations of our guidebooks represent the principal aim of our activities based in the idea to make the attractiveness of Slovakia accessible also to tourists coming from abroad.

The new series **Knapsacked Travel in Slovakia** has been prepared with similar intention. Four books will be published in this series in 2001: The West Tatras (Západné Tatry), The Low Tatras (Nízke Tatry), The Slovak Paradise (Slovenský raj), and The High Tatras (Vysoké Tatry) in four languages: Slovak, English, German, and Polish. As the title of the series suggests, the guidebooks are intended for hikers above all. They contain descriptions of tours, maps illustrating the routes, altitude profiles, classification by exactness and time schedules complemented by photographs of the typical sceneries in most cases. Introduction to the individual books also contains general information, basic characteristics of natural setting of the area in question, and a map of the region with indicated situation of the individual tours. The guidebook also highlights natural landmarks and special points of interests, options to trips, practical information and a register of the most important hiking points.

All recommended tours were written leaning on personal experience of the authors and collaborators. In spite of it, minor changes and discrepancies are possible. We apologize for them and will be grateful if you let us know of any such discrepancy that you may detect. We shall use the information in future editions.

Dear readers,
We are sincerely convinced that you will choose the ideal trip for you from our offer of routes in the most beautiful mountain ranges of Slovakia and will have good time in the romantic setting of the Slovak mountains. We wish you good weather, high spirit and, of course, happy home-coming.

Peter Augustini and Daniel Kollár

Contents

Introduction 3
How to use the guidebook 5
Situation 9
Natural setting 10
Map 24
 1 Across the Starohorské vrchy Mts. 26
 2 The Kozí chrbát Mt. from Donovaly 28
 3 The Kozí chrbát Mt. from Hiadeľ 30
 4 The Veľká Chochuľa Mt. 32
 5 Ráztocké lazy 34
 6 The Ďurková Mt. from Jasenie 36
 7 The ridge of Skalka 38
 8 Around Krpáčovo and Lehoty 40
 9 Around Krpáčovo and Tále 42
10 The Baba Mt. 44
11 The Ďumbier and Chopok Mts. from Trangoška 46
12 The Chopok and Dereše Mts. from Srdiečko 48
13 The Ďumbier Mt. from Mýto pod Ďumbierom 50
14 The Králička Mt. 52
15 The Beňuška Mt. 54
16 From Bacúch to Vyšná Boca 56
17 The Homôľka Mt. 58
18 The Veľká Vápenica Mt. 60
19 The Andrejcová Mt. 62
20 The Kráľova hoľa Mt. from Telgárt 64
21 The Kráľova hoľa Mt. from Liptovská Teplička 66
22 Around Liptovská Teplička 70
23 The Kozí kameň Mt. 72
24 The Veľký bok Mt. 74
25 The Rovná hoľa Mt. 76
26 Instructive path around the river Váh 78
27 The Ohnište Mt. 80
28 The Smrekovica Mt. 82
29 The Ďumbier Mt. from Liptovský Ján 84
30 The Poludnica Mt. 86
31 The Demänovská hora Mt. 88
32 The Demänovská ľadová jaskyňa cave 90
33 The Pusté Mt. 92

34 The Krakova hoľa Mt.	94
35 The Siná a Bôr Mts.	96
36 The Demänovská and Jánska dolina valleys	98
37 Instructive path of the Demänovská dolina valley	100
38 The Chopok Mt. from Jasná	102
39 The Dereše Mt. from Jasná	104
40 The Predná Magura Mt.	106
41 The travertine rocks of Sliač	108
42 The Ďurková Mt. from Magurka	110
43 The Salatín Mt. from Ludrová	112
44 The Salatín Mt. from Železné	114
45 The Brankov Mt. and Brankovský vodopád waterfall	116
46 The Nízke Tatry ridge trail (1st part)	118
47 The Nízke Tatry ridge trail (2nd part)	122
48 The Nízke Tatry ridge trail (3rd part)	126
49 The Nízke Tatry ridge trail (4th part)	128
50 The Nízke Tatry ridge trail (5th part)	130
Natural landmarks and points of interests	133
Registry	142
Dictionary	145
Practical information	146

How to use the guidebook

The series Knapsacked Travel in Slovakia is intended for hikers. The introductory part of the book is dedicated to general information on how to plan the individual trips and the basic principles of movement in nature. The first chapter briefly characterizes the natural conditions (starting with surface forms over the waters, climate, soils, vegetation and wild life, ending by the conservation aspect) of the territory in question. A map of the region in scale 1:500 000, which contains the numbered described hiking routes follows.

Then comes the detailed description of the individual routes. A list of the most important information arranged in entries opens each route description. The first entry is the situation of the territory of the route. The second entry is the starting point with the name of the place where the trip starts and the way how to get there (bus stop of SAD = Slovak Bus Transports or the station of ŽSR which means the Railways of the Slovak Republic, a parking lot). The third entry is the finishing point of the route, the place, where the trip ends and the way how to get from there (again bus stop, railway station or parking lot). The fourth entry contains the schedule and the list of the points of the route accompanied by the time that an average hiker needs get to the next point (the time used for relaxing or sightseeing is not included). The fifth entry is information on altitude difference, i.e. the difference between the lowest and the highest points of the trip. The last entry recommends the map of territory of interest, the hiker should have at hand. They are normally available in the local bookstores or newspaper stalls.

Classification of the tour as to degree of difficulty and description of the basic tour follows. The description emphasizes the landmarks. Part of each route is the cutting of map with outlined course of the tour. Medium demanding and demanding routes are also characterised by the altitude profile while the information is complemented by a photograph illustrating the typical setting. Basic routes are compiled in a way, which includes all important areas of the territory. However, the routes are in no way definite. They are rather recommendations, which can be modified or combined (if you overnight in a mountain hotel, for instance) or shortened. Some trips also contain options.

Classification of trips

The proposed routes run normally on well-marked hiking paths and roads. The hiker is always warned of possible orientation trouble. It means increased attention and frequent use of map. All kinds of hikers — from the experienced and fit ones to the inexperienced and comfort-preferring ones — can choose from our offer. The colour of the route numbers, green, blue or red, express three degrees of the trips: little demanding, moderately demanding and demanding routes.

Easy routes are marked in green and they are suitable for older people, families with children and less fit tourists. They are mostly half-day outings running on good roads or paths with low altitude difference and rather short. Medium demanding tours are marked in blue. They are intended for fit hikers and families with grown-up children. They are longer and the altitude difference is higher. Some of them also require orientation sense and some experience with movement in nature. The red-marked tours are for the above-average hikers in excellent physical condition who are used to all-day walk, high altitude difference, use of climbing aids and difficult orientation, and who possess sufficient experience in movement in difficult terrain.

Outfit

The tours in mountain and high-mountain environment always require an adequate outfit and equipment, suitable clothes and footwear including. Plimsolls or low shoes do not protect against injuries in rocky terrain, especially not on moving debris. Also suitable underwear (special thermo-underwear) is important and the upper Polar garments of different thickness are ideal for unstable weather only too frequent in mountains. Weather-proof jackets and trousers (preferably Goratex made) as the top outfit is recommended as well. You will certainly need a plastic mack, cap, mittens, thermo-isolating foil for emergency situations, and the basic medical kit on long and demanding tours. Ski poles and climbing irons even hatchet are recommended if there are snow fields on the route. You should also carry your ID, a watch, map and guidebook, sufficient food and drinks and a disposal bag (to carry the offal back, do not leave it there). Warm clothes are recommended even in hot summer months as the sudden change of weather can be very unpleasant for a hiker lacking the adequate outfit.

Ten basic principles for safe stay in the mountains
1. Chose the tour fitting your possibilities.
2. Inquire about the chosen tour and its state at the nearest Mountain Rescue Service station.
3. Let your host (person in charge of the establishment where you are accommodated) know about the aim of the tour and expected time of return, and write it in the book of trips before you leave.
4. If you are going away for a longer trip always start in the morning.
5. Your footwear should be solid even in sunny weather.
6. Always have waterproof garments at hand.
7. You should go back if the weather starts to deteriorate.
8. Always stick to the marked trail, do not venture into unknown parts and do not step on snow fields.
9. If the trail above the upper timber line is covered by snow and there are not marking poles in sight, it is considered not marked and you must not continue on it.
10. If you cannot return to the place where you are accommodated, you should notify your host.

Ten basic principles of safe hiking
1. Study the map of your the trip and read the guidebook in advance.
2. Always concentrate on the key points of the routes, especially the crossroads.
3. Abrupt changes of direction or turnings onto less important communications are indicated by a sign (arrow).
4. If you do not find marking in the course of say 300 m where there are enough objects suitable for placing a mark, you have probably gone astray. In that case it is better to go back to the nearest crossroads and find the correct direction.
5. f you are passing through wide open area with hardly discernible paths, please pay attention to the opposite side edge of canopy in case there is a big belt-shaped marking (so-called "tout").

6. There are cases when the rules of marking or the prescribed 3-year interval of renovation of marking were not observed. It can cause poor legibility, insufficient frequency or discrepancy of the marking with regards to the map. Drawbacks are also caused by ploughing away the field roads, building of fences or new forest roads.
7. Look back from time to time and observe the marking running in the opposite direction. It may be more reliable.
8. It is recommendable to measure the distance quoted in the map if you want to calculate the time of the trip and its length.
9. The data on road posts contain information on distances (the first line of the chart quotes the nearest point with road post on the trail, the second and third line inform about important places on the route and the last line quotes the end point).
10. The marked hiking trails are fully utilizable only if there is no snow cover.

Maps

Every route is accompanied by a map with the course of the route. In spite of it, it is recommendable to carry a detailed map issued by VKÚ Harmanec. Particularly, we recommend the series of maps at scale 1:25 000: No. 1 Nízke Tatry — rekreačné strediská, No. 2 Vysoké Tatry — Starý Smokovec, No. 3 Západné Tatry — Podbanské — Zverovka, No. 4 Slovenský raj, No. 6 Donovaly —Šachtička — Turecká, and No. 7 Pieniny.

Transport

The area of the northern Slovakia boasts comparatively thick network of bus lines and in some cases also railway lines. The starting and finishing points of the individual routes are accessible by the collective means of transport. It means that each tour (with the exception of the trips starting and ending at high-mountain cottages or hotels) can be accomplished by going to its starting point by bus or train. The same is applicable with regards to the finishing point.

The Ďumbier Mt.

Situation

The Nízke Tatry Mts. or the Low Tatras spread between the 48°42' and 49°3'of the northern latitude and 19°16' and 19°16' and 20°17' of the eastern longitude. The longer axis of this mountains arranged in belts elongated in the direction of the geometrical parallel is more than 80 km long. The width of the range moves between 15 and 25 km.

The Low Tatras lie almost in the centre of Slovakia. The geographical centre of the country, which is presumably the Hrb Mountain in the northern edge of the volcano from the Tertiary Age called Poľana, is situated only about 14 km from the south-western edge of the mountain range. The northern foothills of the Nízke Tatry Mts. are more than 20 km away from the Slovak-Polish frontier. The southern edge of the range is even more far away from the frontier, about 45 km south-eastward.

The Nízke Tatry Mts. are surrounded by a distinctly lower situated landscape in the north, as well as in the south. It is the Podtatranská kotlina basin in the north and the Horehronské podolie basin in the south. The wide Podtatranská kotlina basin with its flat bottom sharply contrasts with the

The Vajskovská dolina valley

split lateral ridges of the mountains. In the eastern part of the northern foothills of the Low Tatras, between the massive mountain range and basins are the lower Kozie chrbty Mts. The eastern tip of the Hornád basin juts out and touches the range in the north-east. Only the western and eastern neighbours of the Nízke Tatry Mts. are mountains. Their western limit leads through the wide valley of the Revúca river, which separates it from the Veľká Fatra Mts. Further south are the rather low Starohorské vrchy Mts., which were formerly, according to older orographic division, part the Nízke Tatry Mts. Today they are an independent geomorphologic unit. In the east the relief of the range declines into the karstic plateaux of the Slovenský raj Mts.

The Low Tatras formed the frontier of historic regions of the former Kingdom of Hungary and today they limit the administrative and territorial units of the modern Slovak Republic. They separate the region of Horehronie from that of Liptov and western Spiš. Nowadays this distinct natural border also separates the provinces of Žilina, Banská Bystrica and Prešov. The greater part of the northern part of the massif of the Nízke Tatry Mts. is divided between the districts of the province of Žilina: Ružomberok and Liptovský Mikuláš. A small part of it also lies in the territory of the district of Poprad in the province of Prešov. The valleys oriented to the south and the lateral ridges of the mountain range lie in the territory of the districts of province of Banská Bystrica: Banská Bystrica in the west and Brezno in the east. There are 43 towns and villages in the territory of the Nízke Tatry Mts.

Natural setting

Substratum and surface

The geological building of the mountain range is similar to other crystalline-Mesozoic mountain ranges of the Inner Western Carpathians. The central part of the massif consists of crystalline core represented by the

Palaeozoic erupted and transformed rocks. Various types of granite and granodiorite of the Prašivá and Ďumbier type prevail here; smaller forms consist of crystalline schist such as gneiss, amphibolite, and philite. Distribution of the Mesozoic structural units of the mountain range is asymmetrical. The Mesozoic sedimentary rocks are considerably less represented in the south, they are abundant in the north. The Liptov part of the Nízke Tatry Mts. consists prevailingly of limestone and dolomite rocks. The bulky group of strata of the sediments of the tropic Mesozoic Sea is folded and inserted into nappes. The strata of the Krížna nappe, which are seen on the surface in the western and north-western part of the range, consist of softer marl and shale rocks. On these less resistant groups of strata a

The Veľká Vápenica Mt.

lower and smooth-modelled relief will small erosional basins and wide valleys such as the Lužnianska kotlina basin or Revúcke podolie basin (this, however, lies in the neighbouring mountain range of Veľká Fatra Mts.) were formed. Evidently more dramatic reef relief was created on the rocks of the Choč nappe in the northern part of the range east of the Iľanovská dolina valley. Limestone and dolomite rocks, subject to intensive karstification prevail here. The Demänovské vrchy Mts. built mostly of chemically pure Gutenstein limestone rank among the most important karstic areas of Slovakia with unusually developed underground karst. On the other side of the Nízke Tatry Mts., between Moštenica and Mýto pod Ďumbierom in Horehronie region, are only small islands of Mesozoic rocks. The local occurrence of the Mesozoic limestone rocks on the south-eastern slope of the Ďumbier rock with an interesting high-mountain karst also deserves attention. The geological composition of the Nízke Tatry Mts. continues into the neighbouring geomorphologic units, the Starohorské vrchy and Kozie chrbty Mts. Islands of crystalline core with superimposed strata of the young Palaeozoic dry-land sediments can be seen in the Starohorské vrchy Mts. These groups of strata with prevalence of conglomerates were rich in ores in the past.

The view of the Salatín Mt. from the Sivý vrch Mt.

Mining in the Nízke Tatry Mts.

Since the time immemorial the Nízke Tatry Mts. were rich in ores and timber. The forests have retained its wealth until the present day while the ores were extracted and the mining activity almost disappeared. In the past the wider environs of the Nízke Tatry Mts. belonged to the traditional mining regions of Slovakia with rich history in extraction of different ores. In the localities of hydrothermal type copper, iron, antimony, and lead were extracted and the brooks of the mountain range very fairly rich in gold. The principal mining centres were Špania Dolina and Staré Hory, the Krížska dolina valley, Bocianska dolina valley, and Magurka Mt. in the region of Liptov. The mines concentrated in the Horehronie region around the village of Vajsková. Although the miners left the mines of the Nízke Tatry Mts. long ago, traces of their work survive. Huge heaps of deads in Špania Dolina, deposited ore in the eastern slope of the Ďumbier Mt., openings of the galleries around the Magurka Mt. or Korytnica testify to the past. Many of the former mining roads, which served to transport of ore to the smelting plants in Dúbrava, Liptovský Hrádok, Vajsková, Hronec or Podbrezová, are now used by tourists.

The geological building of the depressions next to the Nízke Tatry Mts. is different. The old Tertiary sediments, the remnants of sediments of the sea that covered once a large portion of today's Slovakia including the Nízke Tatry Mts., fill the Podtatranská kotlina basin. The younger Tertiary lake and river sediments cover them in the Horehronské podolie basin.

The Nízke Tatry Mts. is a huge and difficult to pass mountain barrier between the upper Považie and the Horehronie basins. This barrier was originally a wide arc, which later broke into a system of tectonic blocks limited by a system of faults. Uplifting of the range started in the Tertiary era and its altitude increased above the relatively sinking adjacent depressions or lower mountain ranges in the Quaternary Age. The central part of the range was also remodelled by glacier activity in the Quaternary Age.

Tectonic movements uplifted the Nízke Tatry Mts. to the altitude above sea level that makes them the second tallest mountain range in Slovakia and the Western Carpathians. The tallest mountain of the range is Ďumbier (2,043 m). There are another three Low Tatra peaks that are taller than 2,000 m a.s.l. Except for several negligible unnamed mountains not included in the list of peaks, the Nízke Tatry Mts. have 27 mountains taller than 1,700 m, 18 peaks taller than 1,800 m a.s.l. and ten of them reach the altitude above 1,900 m a.s.l.

From the geomorphologic point of view the Nízke Tatry Mts. represent an independent whole, part of the Fatra-Tatra region of the Inner Western Carpathians. They are divided into two sub-wholes and several lower partial geomorphologic units Both sub-wholes acquired the name of their tallest peaks. The Ďumbierske Tatry Mts. are in the west and the Kráľovoholské Tatry are in the east. The border between them leads through the valley of

The peaks of the Nízke Tatry Mts. taller than 1,700 m a.s.l. *(in m)*

1. Ďumbier	2,043.4	15. Baňa	1,859.1
2. Štiavnica	2,025.3	16. Žiarska hoľa	1,840.5
3. Chopok	2,023.6	17. Orlová	1,840.4
4. Dereše	2,003.5	18. Králička	1,807.4
5. Skalka	1,980.1	19. Bartková	1,790.2
6. Chabenec	1,955.0	20. Veľký Gápeľ	1,776.5
7. Kráľova hoľa	1,946.1	21. Veľká Chochuľa	1,753.2
8. Kotliská	1,936.9	22. Krakova hoľa	1,751.6
9. Krúpova hoľa	1,927.5	23. Ďurková	1,749.8
10. Zákľuky	1,914.5	24. Ludárova hoľa	1,731.6
11. Poľana	1,889.7	25. Veľký bok	1,727.1
12. Bôr	1,887.6	26. Rovná hoľa	1,722.9
13. Konské	1,882.3	27. Malá Chochuľa	1,718.6
14. Stredná hoľa	1,875.9		

the Štiavnička to the saddle of Čertovica and continues through the Bocianska and Malužinská dolina valleys.

The Ďumbierske Tatry Mts. is the taller and more dissected part of the Nízke Tatry Mts. Their main ridge is situated in the centre of the range. It runs from the west to the east. Its westernmost part turns southward. Wide alpine meadows and dwarf pine forests cover this arc-formed ridge, which is the axis of the mountain group of Prašivá. It is high above its environs and provides wonderful and far-reaching view. The culminating point of the main ridge is the Veľká Chochuľa Mt. (1,753 m). Two peaks are taller than 1,500 m in the single lateral ridge running to the Horehronie side of the range. The mountain group of Salatíny stands in the north-west of the Ďumbierske Tatry Mts. It consists of a comparatively complicated system of ridges and valleys. The Ludrovská and Ľupčianska dolina valleys are the bulkiest ones. The dominant landscape element is the Salatín Mt. (1,630 m), which gave name to this part of the mountain range. The rocky Salatín, as well as the neighbouring Ľupčianska Magura are separated from the main ridge of the Nízke Tatry Mts. by a belt of lower relief, which was formed on less resistant Mesozoic rocks. A shallow basin, which originated around the Magurka Mt. and Lužnianska kotlina basin is a larger depression situated further in the west.

The greatest natural wealth of the mountain range is the karst; especially varied and developed in the Demänovské vrchy Mts. Geological building of the range predetermines the variety and diversity of this attractive natural phenomenon. The majority of the karstic areas occur in the northern part of the mountains, where it is linked to the wide belt of the Mesozoic sedimentary rocks, such as limestone and dolomite. The individual karstic areas are named after the village, valley or mountain lying nearby. There are the karsts of Demänová, Malužiná, Mošnica, Ľupča, Ludrov, Bystrica, Ďumbier, Staré Hory, Važec, Hybe, Liptovská Teplá, Šumiac, or that of the Jánska dolina valley. The karst of the Nízke Tatry Mts. can be generally characterized as the valley type of karst with better developed underground karst forms than the surface forms. The entrails of the limestone and dolomite massifs contain hundreds of caves of river type. River erosion was the force that formed the cave corridors. The text-book examples of river caves are above all in the Demänová karst where the explorers discovered more than 170 caves. The river Demänovka, which springs in the glacier kettle below the Ďumbier Mt., partially gets lost in underground in the river-glacier high plain of Lúčky. Its water penetrates into the corridors of an intricate cave system in the Demänovská dolina valley. When the water level rises, part of it flows through the surface streams into the lower ponors. The lowest of them is called the Objavný or the Discovery ponor used by explorer J. Král and his companions to enter the underground space when they discovered the Demänovská jaskyňa slobody cave in 1921. The cave is part of an enormous karst system genetically connected with the river Demänovka including the Pustá, Údolná, Jaskyňa pod Útesom, Jaskyňa trosiek,

The Demänovská jaskyňa slobody cave

Vyvieranie, Demänovská jaskyňa mieru, Pavúčia jaskyňa, and Demänovská ľadová jaskyňa caves. The debouchure in the valley of Vyvieranie is the most voluminous one and it is next to the artificial entrance to the Demänovská jaskyňa mieru cave, which is closed to public.

The dream-come-true of cave explorers
The karst of Demänová in the north of the Nízke Tatry Mts. was the scene of fulfilled dreams of cave explorers. A great discovery was accomplished on January 2nd 1987. The success attained by the Slovak cave explorers in the evening of that winter day can be compared with a bit of imagination to the successful meeting of the French and British parts of the Eurotunnel dug under the Dover strait. A group of 58 cave explorers from Ružomberok, Handlová, Rožňava, Terchová, Banská Bystrica, Liptovský Trnovec, Žilina, and Demänovská dolina valley finally found natural connection between the Demänovská jaskyňa mieru cave and the Demänovská jaskyňa slobody cave. The long expected connection of the two greatest caves through the flooded tunnel meant that the total length of the cave system reached 21.5 km. Now it is the longest in Slovakia. The explorers immediately investigated additional hundreds of meters of cave corridors. Today the system of nine genetically con-

Vráta

nected caves in the Demänovská dolina valley is more than 30 km long.

The river Demänovka flows in the lowest situated corridors of the deepest cave system in Demänovská dolina valley. It used to flow higher in the past. At the beginning of the Quaternary Age it flew some hundred metres above its present channel. As the Nízke Tatry Mts. were uplifted by tectonic activity, Demänovka was cutting deeper into the limestone rock. The process took place in several stages and now the explorers can discern as much as nine storeys arranged along the overall depth of 173 metres. Demänovská jaskyňa slobody cave boasts unique drip stone ornamentation, which makes it one of the most beautiful caves of Europe. The overall length of its corridors is more than 8,400 m, out of which 1,145 have been surveyed to date. There are numerous large hollow spaces in this cave called halls and domes with wonderful sinters. Veľký dóm or the Large Dome with dimensions 75x45x65 m is the largest of them. Apart from several stretches of underground channel of the Demänovka the visitors can also see the cave lakes. The big lake is as much as 52 m long and 7 m deep. In Demänovská jaskyňa cave there is a permanent temperature of 6.1 to 7.0 degrees Celsius all over the year. High relative air humidity of 94 to 99 percent is suitable for therapy. Diseases of the upper respiratory tract and allergies are successfully cured here. Another cave open to the public is in the lower part of the Demänovská dolina valley. This cave has been known since the Middle Ages and it is the second largest of its kind in Slovakia. The ice filing of this cave presumably originated some 400 to 500 years ago. The Demänovská ľadová jaskyňa cave is also known for the bones of cave bear, which were taken for remnants of some drake in the 18th century. There live seven species of bats in this cave. Out of 1,750 m of cave corridors 850 are open to the public. On the eastern side of the Demänovská dolina valley is another remarkable cave called Okno or Window at the altitude of 150 m above the river Demänovka. Parallel with the Demänovská dolina valley lies the Jánska dolina valley heading to the east. This valley is also rich in karstic phenomena. There are numerous caves, ponors, springs, and sinkholes. In the lower part of the same valley is the Stanišovská jaskyňa cave, one of the oldest in the Nízke Tatry Mts. In the slope of the Krakova hoľa Mt. (1,761 m) lies the entrance into the Starý hrad cave 432 m deep. The Ľadová priepasť abyss in the opposite mountain of Ohnište (1,533 m) is also interesting. An enormous ice cone jams its lower part.

Six tall mountains including the Ďumbier Mt. (2,043 m) are concentrated in the Ďumbier mountain group, the tallest in the Nízke Tatry Mts. Except for one, all of them are within the main ridge, which leads from the Sedlo pod Skalkou saddle (1,476 m) in the west to the Čertovica saddle (1,238 m) in the east. The main ridge has numerous lateral ridges, which alternate with huge valleys. The tallest of them is Skalka (1,980 m) which starts in Kotliská (1,936 m) and runs southward. The northern lateral ridges, which end further in the north in the karstic Demänovské vrchy Mts., are longer and rocky. The beauty and interesting shape of some mountains in the northern lateral ridges such as the Siná (1,500 m), Krakova hoľa (1,751 m), and Ohnište (1,533 m) call attention for their remarkable rock galleries and the famous rock window. The transversal profile of the slopes of the man ridge is distinctly asymmetrical. Concave slopes covered by alpine meadows and in places by extensive debris fields decline on their southern side, while

The Važecká jaskyňa

The longest caves in the Nízke Tatry Mts. *(in m)*

System of Demänovské jaskyne caves	more than 30,000
Jaskyňa Zlomísk cave (Jánska dolina valley)	10,370
Jaskyňa mŕtvych netopierov cave (Trangoška)	8,000
Jaskyňa Starý hrad cave (Jánska dolina valley)	5,101
Jaskyňa v Záskočí cave (Jánska dolina valley)	5,034

the northern side consists prevailingly of steep rock faces divided into troughs and ribs. The cause of this phenomenon is irregular glaciation of the Low Tatras, which took place in the glacial era of the older Quaternary Age. The northern valleys were more glaciated and typical glacier kettles or cirques with flat bottoms and steep slopes were modelled here. The southern side of the range was covered by less and smaller glaciers. There were 16 valley and cirque glaciers in the whole territory of the Nízke Tatry Mts. The Krížňanský glacier 6,050 m long was the longest of them. The glacier in the valley of Štiavnica was only 350 m shorter. The bulkiest glacier on the southern side of the range in the Bystrá dolina valley was 5 km long.

The eastern part of the Nízke Tatry Mts. is occupied by the geomorphologic sub-whole called the Kráľovohoľské Tatry Mts. The main ridge of this part of the range is situated close to the river Hron in the south. This is the reason why the southern lateral ridges and valleys are shorter than the northern. The western part of the Kráľovohoľské Tatry Mts. consists of an extensive group of mountains called **Priehyba**. Its main ridge is comparatively low and in places it drops below the upper timberline. It rises to the belt of alpine meadows only in the area of the Homôľka (1,659 m), Veľké Vápenice (1,691 m) and Andrejcová (1,519 m) mountains. The lowest point of the whole ridge of the Nízke Tatry Mts., the saddle of Priehyba (1,189 m) is also here. No road leads through this saddle and the only place where it is possible to pass the range is the about 40 higher lying saddle of Čertovica (1,238 m) on the divide between the Ďumbierske and Kráľovohoľské Tatry Mts. In the Priehyba mountain group the Veľký bok (1,727 m), a wide mountain calls attention. This massive mountain taller than those around him used to have on its northern side a small cirque glacier in the glacial era. Dangerous avalanches are falling down its smooth slopes in winter. In the Žiarske sedlo saddle (1,473 m) the main ridge enters the territory of the mountain group called Kráľova hoľa. The easternmost part of the mountain range culminates by the Kráľova hoľa Mt (1,946 m). Small stones cover its top with the TV tower. This concave mountain of monumental shape is an important landscape dominant of this part of Slovakia. The Kráľova hoľa Mt. mentioned in numerous legends and praised by uncountable songs and poems is, along with the High Tatra peak Kriváň, the symbol of Slovak patriotism.

The deepest caves in the Nízke Tatry Mts. (in m)

Jaskyňa Starý hrad cave (Jánska dolina valley)	432
Javorová priepasť abyss (Jánska dolina valley)	312
Jaskyňa mŕtvych netopierov cave (Trangoška)	300
Jaskyňa v Záskočí cave (Jánska dolina valley)	284
System of Demänovské jaskyne caves (Demänovská dolina valley)	173

At the Veľký bok Mt.

On the southern side of the massif of the Kráľova hoľa are shorter slopes dissected by small valleys. On the northern side, which was covered by three small glaciers in the glacial age, are long forested ridges and valleys. Part of the valleys concentrate into the shallow Teplická kotlina basin. East of it lies rather short marginal mountain group of the Nízke Tatry Mts., **Predná hoľa.** The tallest mountain of the forested highland Čertovica reaches the altitude above sea level of 1,427 m.

The Starohorské vrchy Mts. and Kozie chrbty Mts. were also part of the Nízke Tatry Mts. according to older geomorphologic division. Today they are classified as independent geomorphologic wholes of the regions of Fatra-Tatra. The **Starohorské vrchy Mts.** lie south-west of the Low Tatra mountain group called Prašivá. The tallest mountains of the forested highland stand on its north-eastern edge. On a short crest west of the Hiadeľské sedlo saddle (1,099 m) is the tallest mountain of **Kozí chrbát** (1,330 m). A more developed valley network is situated south of the valley of the Hron. The Starohorská dolina valley, which is the access to the mountain saddle of Donovaly (960 m), is the bulkiest one. Short valleys ending in the larger Korytnická dolina valley are turned to the north. The Kozie chrbty Mts. in the north-east represent a kind of foreland to the higher Kráľovohoľské Tatry

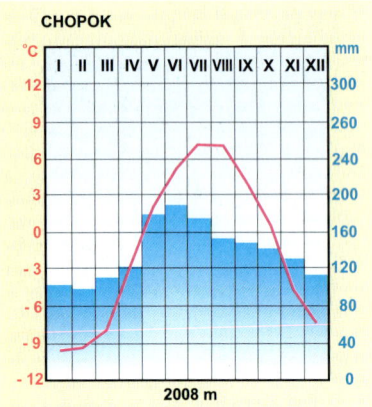

Monthly temperatures and precipitation

Mts. They create a narrow mountain barrier between the rivers of Čierny and Biely Váh. Further to the east Kozie chrbty Mts. slightly widen and rise. In their middle is the tallest peak of the range **Kozí kameň Mt**. (1,255 m). And further to the east the mountain ridge tapers and enters between the Popradská kotlina basin in the north and the Vikartovská priekopa graben of the Hornádska kotlina basin.

Climate and waters

The tourists must count on harsh mountain climate in the Nízke Tatry Mts. The high-mountain parts of the range lying above the upper timber line are the coldest and most humid and also most windy. The temperature changes with the increasing altitude above sea level. The mean January temperature –8 °C and in July not more than mean 9 °C was measured on the crests. The annual average, for instance on top of the Chopok Mt., does not surpass 0 °C. In the valley the temperature is somewhat more friendly with mean January temperatures around –6 °C and the mean July temperature 14 °C. In sub-mountain areas and at the foothills of the mountains it is even better with the mean January temperature -5 °C.

The altitude above sea level and position within the mountain range also determine the rainfall. The mean annual average precipitation is under 900 mm in lower positions. Precipitation is more abundant on the north-western side of the range. The annual precipitation total of Staré Hory, for example, with the altitude above sea level 486 m is 1,048, approximately the same amount as in the village of Jarabá further to the east lying in the altitude 823 m a.s.l. Staré Hory is situated on the windward and Jarabá lies leeward of the range and the prevailing direction of the humid air currents. The greatest amount of precipitation falls at the summits, the annual total of the Chopok Mt. is as much as 1,600 m while the major part of it falls as snow. Snow cover at the Chopok Mt. lasts the long 130 days, in the northern glacier kettles it is even more than 200 days. For comparison, the landscape in the Liptovská kotlina basin is covered by snow for about 60 days. Snow avalanches are very dangerous for winter tourists and skiers. They occur on steep slopes and in troughs on the periphery of the glacier kettles. The best months for winter trekking and skiing are April or May when the snow cover is more stabilized. However, the weather instability and frequent thunderstorms threaten the summer hikers. The best time for hiking is autumn. During the period called the Indian summer the temperatures are lower, but the weather is stable and dry. The only relative disadvantage are shorter days, a thing to take into account when planning longer trips. Atmospheric inversions, which occur in the autumn and winter months makes the trips to the main ridge more attractive as the surrounding depressions are submerged in thick mist while the summits are bathing in sun rays.

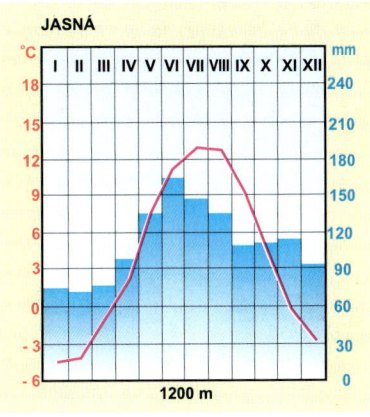

Monthly temperatures and precipitation

The Nízke Tatry Mts. constitute a divide between the basin of the Váh in the north and that of the Hron in the south. Only a small part of the range in the group of mountains of Predná hoľa in the east is part of the Hornád basin. The Kráľova hoľa Mt. represents an important dividing point, which is often referred to as the "roof" of Slovakia. Four great Slovak rivers spring in its slopes: the Čierny Váh, Hornád, Hnilec, and Hron. In the north-western part of the range is a parallel river network formed by comparatively little branched brooks. The largest of them are: Demänovka, Lupčianka, Paludžanka, and Štiavnica. A specific feature of this region is the existence of underground channels of the brooks flowing in karstic landscape of the Demänovské vrchy Mts. The water debouches in several points, for instance, in Demänovská and Jánska doliny valleys. East of the Bocianska dolina valley the river network is a bit different. The main water divide is shifted further to the south creating space of a branched, tree-like network of brooks. The river network unites here into the Čierny Váh river that carries the water to the Liptovská kotlina basin. On the Horehronie side of the Nízke Tatry Mts. a network of parallel brooks mouthing in the Hron originated. The greatest brooks in the western and central part of the southern side are: the Bystrianka, Štiavnička, Vajskovský potok, Lomnistá, and Jaseniansky potok brooks. Short brooks such as Šumiacky potok brook on the southern slopes of the Kráľová hoľa Mt. are in the east. Some streams have an uneven longitudinal profile with several waterfalls. Brankovský vodopád waterfall in the mountain group of Salatíny is the fourth highest in Slovakia. It is 55 m

The Ďumbier Mt.

high but it is often short of water. The Martalúska waterfall in the spring part of the Hnilec on the slope of the Kráľova hoľa Mt. is five metres shorter. In the Vajskovská dolina valley is the 30 m high cascade. Small waterfalls are in the environs of the Korytnica, in the Hučiaky valley below the Salatín, in the little side valley of Machnatô in the Demänovská dolina valley and near Vyšná Boca in the Svidkovská dolina valley. There are not so many lakes in the Nízke Tatry Mts. as in the High Tatras. The Vrbické pleso lake is a unique natural water reservoir in the Demänovská dolina valley. It lies in the altitude 1,113 m above sea level and its area is 6.2 ha. Mineral springs occur mostly in marginal fault systems in the periphery of the Nízke Tatry Mts. A medicinal spring is in Korytnica. The hot spring in Liptovský Ján feeds the local swimming pool. More mineral springs of local importance finds one in Mýto pod Ďumbierom, Magurka, Železnô, Bacúch, Pohorelá, and in Jasenianska, Hiadeľská, and Moštenická dolina valleys.

Soil, vegetation and wild life

The Low Tatras contain three different landscape types: forest, alpinemeadow, and cliff type. The forest type is the most spread one. Forest stands occupy as much as 90 percent of the area. Forest associations are arranged in altitude belts. Beach trees mixed with spruce trees grow above all in lower positions. Oak stands are spread around Brezno. Extensive spruce forests, which grow in the sea level altitude 1,150 m in the northern side and 1,300 m in the southern part of the range are above the belt of beach. They reach as high as the upper timber line. The forests grow mostly on the cambisol on acid substratum and rendzinas are the soils, which thrive on carbonate substratum. The shepherds lowered the upper timber line below the present 1,500 m above sea level. Dwarf pine forest grows only on 0.3 percent of the area of the National Park of the Nízke Tatry Mts. today. Alpine meadows called here "hole" occupy a considerably larger area. Shallow soil of litosol and ranker types are spread here. Herb vegetation is varied on the northern side ridges on limestone and dolomite substratum. The massifs of Salatín (1,630 m), Siná (1,560 m), Krakova hoľa (1,751 m), and Ohnište (1,533 m) are covered by colourful flora with some rare plants such as *Pulsatilla slavica*, and the glacial relic dryad. The cliffs of the northern valleys of the mountain range such as in the Demänovské vrchy Mts. and the Salatíny represent a special landscape type. Apart from spruce, the original pine and maple tree and other debris type of wood species grow here.

The wild life of the Nízke Tatry Mts. is unusually varied. Red deer, boar, wolf, fox live here. The symbol of the mountain range is the bear.

The Ohnište Mt.

The bear, symbol of the Nízke Tatry Mts.
Perhaps the most popular mammal of the Nízke Tatry Mts. is the bear, which is also depicted in the badge of the National Park. There are about 160 individuals living in the forests of the range. The number of bears is controlled in spite of occasional problems with them. Although they have got enough food in their natural environment sometimes, they draw closer to human settlements to look for food. This is how the tourists can spot sometimes a bear-family having a feast near some of the hotels in Demänovská dolina valley, for instance. The Jánska dolina valley is also famous for unexpected encounters between the tourists and a roaming bear, which does not always end in nervous flee of the disturbed animal back into the thick wood. Black chronicles also describe cases, which ended up in hospital in Liptovský Mikuláš.

Nature conservation

The natural values of the Nízke Tatry Mts. have been protected for more than two decades now. The National Park of the Nízke Tatry Mts. (NAPANT), which also includes the territory of the neighbouring geomorphologic wholes the Starohorské vrchy Mts., Horehronské podolie basin and the Kozie chrbty Mts. was established in 1978, but the history of nature conservation in this part of Slovakia started much earlier. The original area of

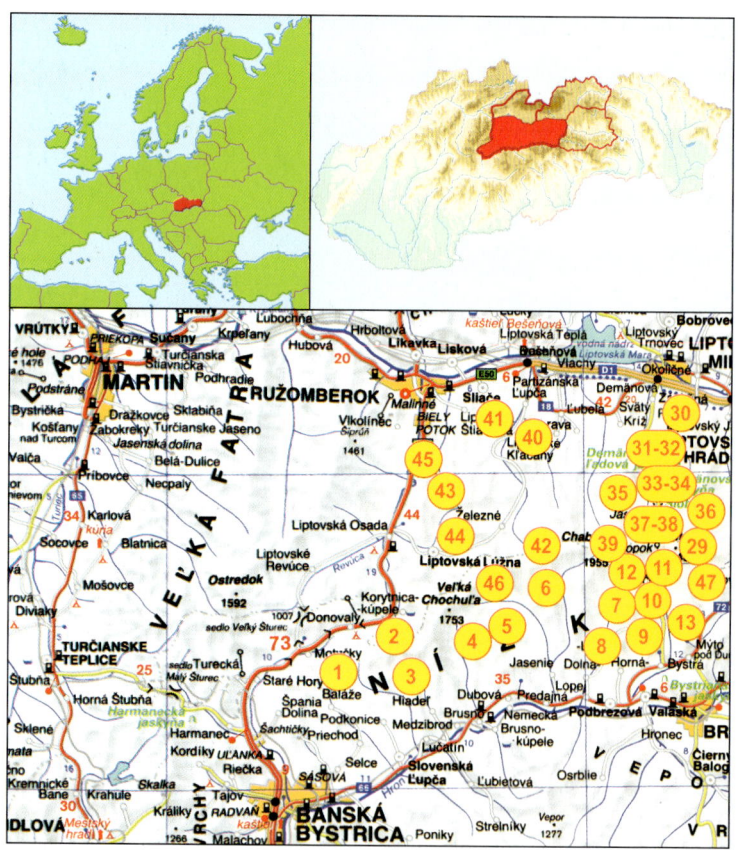

the NAPANT was 82,095 hectares plus the protective belt on 123,990 hectares. In 1997 the limits of the National Park were widened in order to attain better protection of the territory. Now the territory of the NAPANT lies on an area 72,842 ha and the protective belt occupies 110,162 ha and it makes it the largest National Park in Slovakia. The NAPANT borders on the National Park of the Slovenský raj Mts. in the east. Out of the total area of the National Park 61 percent is owned by the state, the rest is private or

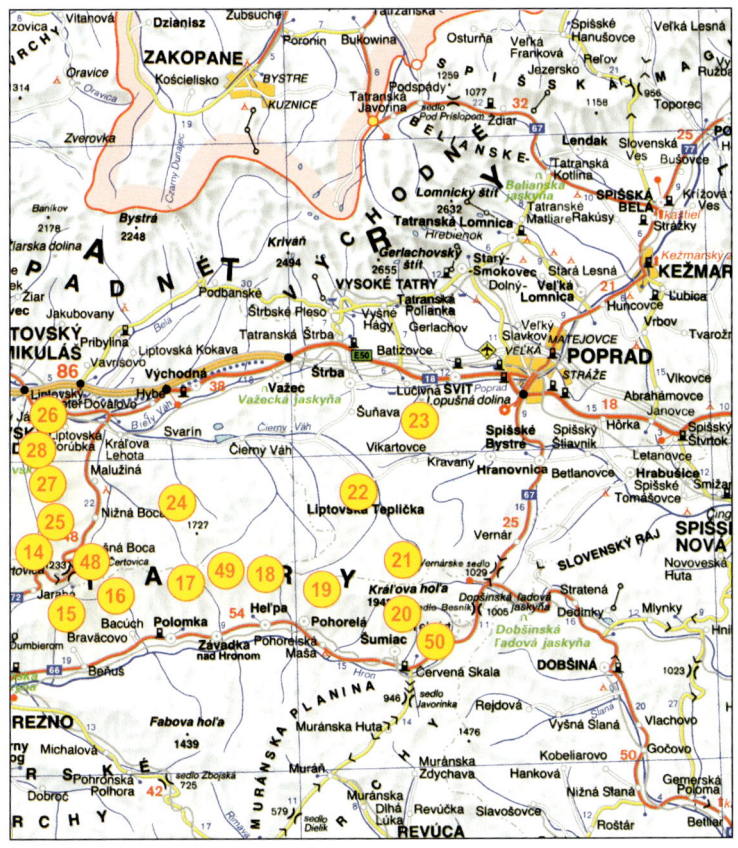

communal property. Almost 10,000 ha of the territory, or 6 percent of the total area of NAPANT falls under stricter protection in form of small-area protected territories. There are eleven national nature reserves, eleven nature reserves, five national nature phenomena, six nature phenomena and two protected areas. The Nature Reserve of Skalka on an area 2,659.81 ha is the largest of them.

1 Across the Starohorské vrchy Mts.

Donovaly – Bully – Pod Jelenskou skalou – Šachtička – Špania Dolina

Situation: The Starohorské vrchy Mts.
Starting point: Donovaly, bus stop, parking lot.
Finishing point: Špania Dolina, bus stop, parking lot.
Time schedule: Donovaly – Bully ½ h – Pri javore ¼ h – Kováčová 1 h – Pod Jelenskou skalou ¾ h – Horný Šturec ½ h – Šachtička ¾ h – Špania Dolina ½ h
Total: 4 ¾ hours.
Elevation gain: 330 m.
Map: Okolie Banskej Bystrice – Donovaly 1 : 50 000 (sheet 100), VKÚ, š. p., Harmanec.

Classification: Undemanding, easy and comfortable outing with low altitude difference. The marking of instructive path improves orientation.

Basic route: The route follows the instructive path of Donovaly-Šachtička. Start at **Donovaly** (980 m) going southward up asphalt road running on the western edge of ski tracks. Abandon the red mark (E8, 0801) at Vrchlúka turning right onto the green mark (5429). Walking on asphalt road you will get to the upper end of the settlement **Bully** (1,005 m). Continue on field road, which ascends shortly after to the crossroads next to the spring **Pri Javore** (1,040 m). The instructive path along with the

Špania Dolina

green mark turns right at the crossroads avoiding the Hrubý vrch Mt. (1,169 m) from the right. Forests alternate with meadows in picturesque and little dissected landscape. The route again avoids the elevation of Krčahy (1,129 m) from the south and later also the Koškov vrch Mt. (1,131 m). It does not ascend to Jelenská skala rock (1,153 m) either. One can climb it from the meadow **Pod Jelenskou skalou** (1,020 m) by turning right onto unmarked path. Continue from the meadow in a slightly declining terrain in thick beech forest. Under the Žiar Mt. (1,045 m) at the saddle **of Horný Šturec** is the crossroads. Yellow mark bending to the right leads to the saddle of Dolný Šturec and further to Staré Hory. Your green mark leads you southward as far as the saddle of **Šachtička** (950 m). After refreshment in the local mountain hotel the final stretch of the tour comes. Abandon the route of instructive path, which follows the blue mark to the quarter of Banská Bystrica, Sásová. Turn right sticking to the green and blue marks. Steep stony road will carry you to **Špania Dolina** (710 m). The village situated in the head of the Banská dolina valley is the wonderful conclusion of this pleasant trip. It offers plenty of interesting landmarks and monuments of its rich mining history.

Options: You can also finish the trip in Banská Bystrica at the quarter of Sásová. Leave the basic route at Šachtička turning left onto the blue mark (in total 5 ¼ hours).

2 The Kozí chrbát Mt. from Donovaly

Donovaly – Kečka – Kozí chrbát – Hiadeľské sedlo – Korytnica-kúpele

Situation: The Starohorské vrchy Mts.
Starting point: Donovaly, bus stop, parking lot.
Finishing point: Korytnica-kúpele, bus stop, parking lot.
Time schedule: Donovaly – Polianka ½ h – Kečka 1 ¼ h – Kozí chrbát 1 h – Hiadeľské sedlo ½ h – Pod Babou ½ h – Korytnica-kúpele ½ h
Total: 4 ¼ hours.
Elevation gain: 500 m.
Map: Okolie Banskej Bystrice – Donovaly 1 : 50 000 (sheet 100), VKÚ, š. p., Harmanec.

Classification: Undemanding, easy and comfortable trip with good orientation. It does not reach the high-mountain zone.
Basic route: Start at **Donovaly** (980 m) going to south and follow the red hiking marks. The first stretch coincides with the Cesta hrdinov SNP road (E8, 0801), covering part of the ridge of the Nízke Tatry Mts. tour (see tour No. 46). Asphalt road slightly ascends to the slope on the western edge of the ski tracks below the Baník Mt. Cart road heads to the village of **Polianka** (1,043 m). Then the trail runs on slightly steeper forest road ascending to the forested slope of the plain of **Barania hlava** (1,101 m). The plain more or less maintains the altitude of 1,030 m above sea level. The route slightly drops to the shallow grassy **Moštenické sedlo** saddle (1,050 m) lying on the edge of the plain. Short steep ascent to the **Kečka Mt.** (1,225 m) follows. The open grassy landscape with wonderful views will accompany you on the tallest ridge of the Starohorské vrchy Mts. as far as the Hiadeľské sedlo sad-

The Kozí chrbát Mt.

dle. Marked path will carry you across the tallest mountain of the mountain range, **Kozí chrbát Mt.** (1,330 m) and then it drops to the **Hiadeľské sedlo** saddle (1,099 m) at the border of the Starohorské vrchy Mts. and the Nízke Tatry Mts. In case of bad weather you can avoid the Kozí kameň Mt. traversing its northern slope. The traverse, which also leads to the Hiadeľské sedlo saddle, is marked in yellow (8432). You will leave the ridge trail at the saddle turning left onto the blue mark (2623). The route does not lead to the deep valley of Barborina dolina. It traverses the western slope of the massive mountain of Prašivá. This long stretch almost coincides with contour line. It cuts several steep valleys called Úplazy. The tablet commemorating the parachute intervention during the Slovak National Uprising in 1944 is situated within short distance from the Hiadeľské sedlo saddle. Passing the Predný úplaz the route slightly descends and reaches the **Sedlo pod Babou** saddle (949 m). There are cottages and ski lift in the saddle. A short detour leads to the **Baba Mt.** (1,120 m). An unmarked path leads to it. Leave the saddle following the blue-marked forest road, which leads to the head of the **Medokýšna dolina** valley, which will comfortably carry you to the aim at the **Korytnica-kúpele** spa (830 m). The mineral springs of this spa village offer refreshment to hikers.

3 The Kozí chrbát Mt. from Hiadeľ

Hiadeľ – Hiadeľské sedlo – Kozí chrbát – Kyslá – Moštenica

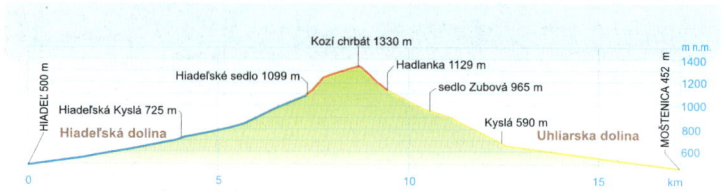

Situation: The Starohorské vrchy Mts.
Starting point: Hiadeľ, bus stop, parking lot.
Finishing point: Moštenica, bus stop, parking lot.
Time schedule: Hiadeľ - Hiadeľská kyslá 1 h - Hiadeľské sedlo 1 ¼ h - Kozí chrbát ¾ h - Hadlanka ¼ h - Zubová ½ h - Kyslá ½ h - Moštenica 1 h.
Total: 5 ¼ hours.
Elevation gain: 878 m.
Map: Okolie Banskej Bystrice - Donovaly 1 : 50 000 (sheet 100), VKÚ, š. p., Harmanec

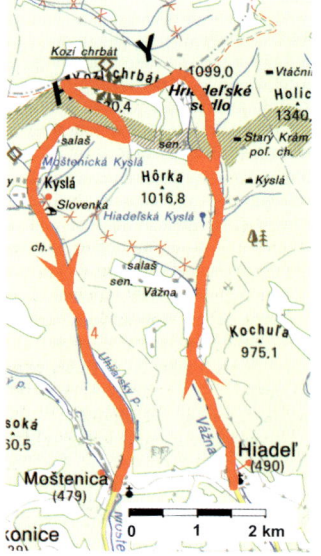

Classification: Medium difficult tour with demanding stretch including the ascent to Hiadeľské sedlo saddle and further to the Kozí chrbát Mt.
Basic route: Start at the final bus stop at the upper end of the village of **Hiadeľ** (500 m). The whole ascent to the Hiadeľské sedlo saddle is marked in blue (2623). You will get to the **Hiadeľská dolina** valley on firm asphalt road. At the end of the lateral valley the road passes by the gamekeeper's lodge of Vážna standing in the forest left of the road. About a kilometre beyond the gamekeeper's lodge is a minerals spring of **Hiadeľská kyslá** (725 m) offering fresh acid water. Next to the monument to the victims of the Slovak National Uprising at the **Prostredný grúň** (800 m) the route abandons the bottom of the valley via long switchback in the eastern slope and then it ascends to a steep forested ridge. Reaching the axis of the ridge

The Hiadeľská dolina valley

abandon the road turning left onto a waterlogged farm track. Ascending in it you will arrive at the grassy **Hiadeľské sedlo** saddle (1,099 m). Continue in the saddle in the opposite direction like in tours Nos. 2 and 46. Following the red mark (E8, 0801) you will ascend to the top of the **Kozí chrbát Mt.** (1,330) with beautiful view of the Starohorské vrchy Mts. and the group of Prašivá in the Nízke Tatry Mts. You can also get to the **crossroads** at the **Hadlanka** saddle (1,129 m) behind the Kozi chrbát Mt. avoiding the tallest mountain of the Starohorské vrchy Mts. if you traverse its northern slope. Turn left at the crossroads and following the yellow mark (8432) and oblique traverse this time in the southern slope of the Kozi chrbát Mt., descend to the saddle **of Zubová** (965 m). The route continues from the saddle almost in the opposite direction. It descends abruptly in the head of the Uhliarska dolina valley first in the forest and then in meadows as far as the **Jegorov prameň** spring (655 m). A little detour to the travertine terraces of the **natural phenomenon of Moštenické travertíny** is certainly interesting. Walking to it pass by the **Na Kanceľ** spring. Asphalt road in valley leads from the Jegorov prameň spring along the cottages of the recreation settlement called **Kyslá** (590 m). About half an hour comfortable walk down the Uhliarska dolina valley will carry you to the village of **Moštenica** (452 m) where the trip ends.

4 The Veľká Chochuľa Mt.

Brusno – Sopotnická dolina – Veľká Chochuľa – Ráztocká hoľa – Ráztoka

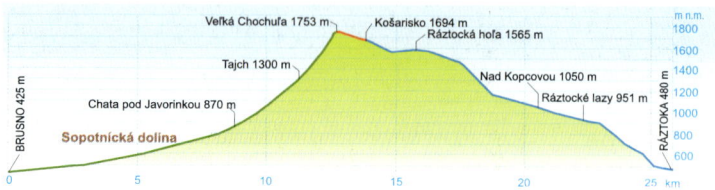

Situation: The Nízke Tatry Mts. – South (western part).
Starting point: Brusno, bus stop, parking lot.
Finishing point: Ráztoka, bus stop, railway station, parking lot.
Time schedule: Brusno - Chata pod Javorinkou 2 ½ h - Tajch ¾ h - Veľká Chochuľa 1 h - Košarisko ¼ h - Ondrejská hoľa ½ h - Ráztocká hoľa ½ h - Nad Kopcovou 1 ¼ h - Ráztocké lazy ¼ h - Ráztoka ¾ h. **Total:** 7 ¾ hours.
Elevation gain: 1 328 m.
Map: Okolie Banskej Bystrice - Donovaly 1 : 50 000 (sheet 100), VKÚ, š. p., Harmanec.

Classification: Strenuous and difficult all-day high-mountain tour with high altitude difference. The shortest return trip is that from the ridge back to the Sopotnická dolina valley.
Basic route: The railway station at **Brusno** (452 m) where the trip starts lies on the left bank of the river Hron. Cross the bridge over the river following the green marks (5442). Continue under the main road and on asphalt road up the **Sopotnická dolina** valley. The asphalt road leads as far as the **Chata pod Javorinkou** hunter's cottage (870 m) where it links with forest road. Below the next **chata Tajch** hunter's cottage (1,300 m) the route abandons the bottom of the valley and ascends up the beech forest. Shortly after you will enter deforested terrain where you have to pay attention to the marking on stones and posts or dwarf pine trees as the path disappears in places. The ascent becomes steeper above the zone of dwarf pine trees. Ascend to the shallow saddle and then to the main ridge west of the main top of the **Veľká Chochuľa Mt.** (1,753 m). Continue from the beautiful top within the ridge of Prašivá on ridge path marked in red hiking marks (E8, 0801). This is the Cesta hrdinov SNP path and you will leave it soon because at the crossroads **Košarisko** (1,694 m) you will have to turn right onto the blue-marked path (2622). The path slightly descends on deforested crest of the tall lateral ridge of the Ondrejská and Ráztocká hoľa Mts. It passes through clearings in dwarf pine stands. The path avoids the **Ondrejská hoľa Mt.**

(1,592 m). It maintains south of the lateral ridge. A secondary marking leads from the road post to the top of the **Ráztocká hoľa Mt.** (1,565 m). Its top offers a fine view of the main ridge of the Low Tatry Mts. Return back to the road post and ascend from the lateral ridge to the south-eastern side. Steep descent will bring you down to the forest belt. The path becomes milder at **Polianky** and the route of the descent heads along the ridge to the scarcely distinct elevation of **Matúšová** (1,176 m) and passes by its left side.

Yellow mark, which ends in the village of Pohronský Bukovec, diverges to the right at the crossroads at the sedlo **Nad Kopcovou** saddle (1,050 m). On the opposite side of the crossroads in a shallow depression is the round grassy ridge offering nice views. Descend from the saddle following the blue mark to the **Ráztocké lazy meadows** (951 m). The road descends down the round step-like ridge between meadows and fields. When it passes by sand pit it turns left and heads down the slope to the village of **Ráztoka** (480 m). In case there is no bus connection you can continue walking to Nemecká (about ¾ hour) where there is better bus connection and railway station. As soon as you get on the main road you can also have a look at the local monument to the heroes of the Slovak National Uprising.

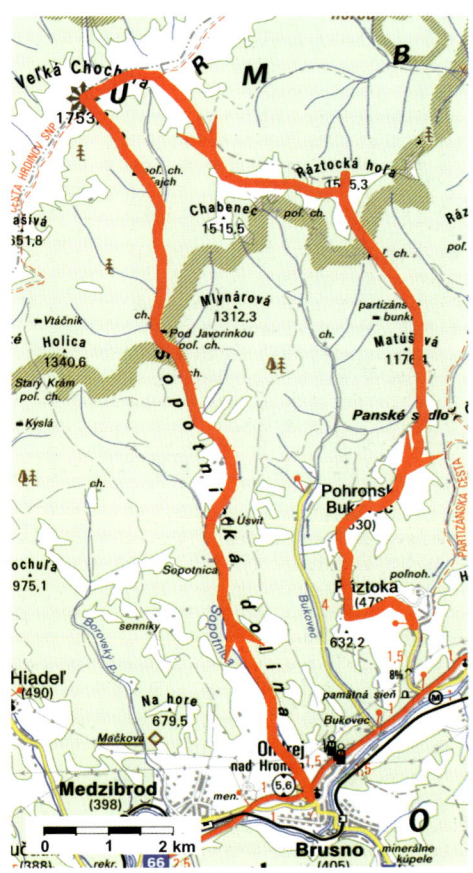

5 Ráztocké lazy

Pohronský Bukovec – Ráztocké lazy – Panské sedlo – Nemecká

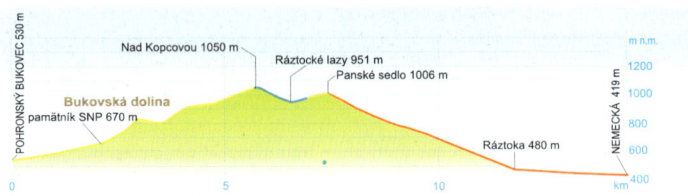

Situation: The Nízke Tatry Mts. – South (western part), Horehronské podolie basin
Starting point: Pohronský Bukovec, bus stop, parking lot.
Finishing point: Nemecká, bus stop, railway station, parking lot.
Time schedule: Pohronský Bukovec - Památnik SNP ¾ h - Nad Kopcovou 1 ¼ h - Ráztocké lazy ¼ h - Nad Kopcovou ¼ h - Panské sedlo ¼ h - Ráztoka 1 h - Nemecká 1 h.
Total: 4 ¾ hours.
Elevation gain: 631 m.
Map: Okolie Banskej Bystrice - Donovaly 1 : 50 000 (sheet 100), VKÚ, š. p., Harmanec.

Classification: Moderately difficult half-day trip with comparatively high altitude difference. Orientation is easy and the trip does not reach the high-mountain altitude above the upper timber line.

Basic route: Start next to the mineral spring in the village of **Pohronský Bukovec** (530 m) following the yellow mark (8451) up the **Bukovská dolina** valley. Stopping at the municipal office you can read the tablet on its wall, which commemorates that the Nazi soldiers burned down this village in 1945. In 1944 the German troops took prisoners the Slovak Generals Golián and Viest, the leaders of the Slovak National Uprising in this village. Cart road leads along the valley bottom around gamekeeper's lodge to the **monument of the Slovak National Uprising,** which commemorates the presence of the parachute brigade of A. S. Jegorov in this valley. Also the next stop near the reconstructed partisan bunkers (900 m) in the Matúšová dolina valley are the reminders of the tumultuous events in 1944. Leaving the bunkers the path continues traversing the

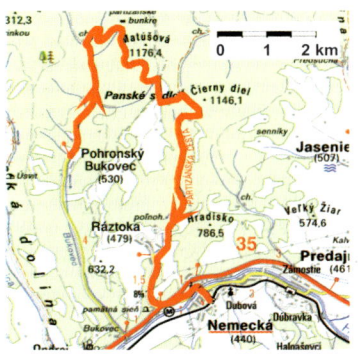

The Prašivá Mt.

forested western slope of the Matúšová Mt. (1,176 m) and heads to the crossroads at the **Nad Kopcovou** saddle (1,050 m). The grassy ridge south-east of the saddle provides a fine view of the region of Horehronie. You will get more views of the surrounding landscape if you follow the blue mark (2622) leading to the **Ráztocké lazy** (951 m). Go back to the crossroads then. Turning to the east you will get to a short hiking link marked in yellow. It will carry you to the **Panské sedlo** saddle (1,006 m). Red-marked hiking path (0816) also called Partizánska cesta (Partisan's Road) connecting the villages of Nemecká and Tále runs through the saddle. Turn right and use this section of the road, which descends to the south. The route coincides with the forest road in waterlogged meadows in the upper part of the descent. It continues around a spring near the hunter's cottage and turns down to the valley of the Ráztocký potok brook. Continue descending along the brook and you will arrive at the village of **Ráztoka** (480 m). Pass along the eastern edge of the village and go down the road to **Nemecká** (419 m). Before arriving at the village you will pass by another **monument to the SNP**. Part of the monument is the former lime kiln, where the Nazi troops massacred more than 600 local civilians. The trip ends at the railway station on the other bank of the Hron river.

6 The Ďurková Mt. from Jasenie

Jasenie – Lomnistá dolina – Ďurková – Jasenianska dolina – Jasenie

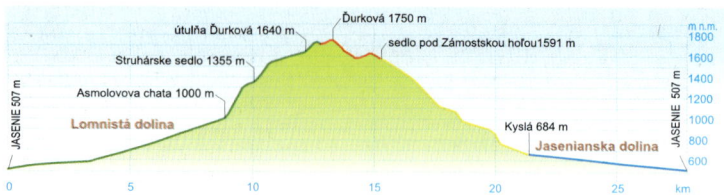

Situation: The Nízke Tatry Mts. – South (western part).
Starting and finishing point: Jasenie, bus stop, parking lot.
Time schedule: Jasenie - Lomnistá dolina-crossroads ¾ h - Struhárske sedlo 1 ½ h - Sedlo Ďurková 1 h - Ďurková ¼ h - Zámostská hoľa 1 h - Kyslá 1 ½ h - Predsuchá 1 ¼ h - Jasenie ¼ h
Total: 8 hours.
Elevation gain: 1,243 m.
Map: Nízke Tatry - Chopok 1 : 50 000 (sheet 122), VKÚ, š. p., Harmanec.

Classification: Difficult and strenuous all-day high-mountain tour with high altitude difference. In case of bad weather you can descend rapidly to Magurka on the northern side of the mountain range.
Basic route: Start at the village of **Jasenie** (507 m) and follow the green hiking mark (5609) up the valley. Before crossing the bridge over the brook beyond the village is the crossroads **V Lomnistej doline** where you turn right and continue to the Lomnistá dolina valley. The road leads on the right bank of the Lomnistá brook passing by the Lomnistá hotel, a swimming pool and cottage settlement on the other side of the brook. A short section of the route up to the next crossroads coincides with what is called Partizánska cesta or Partisan's road marked in red (0816). Turn left at the next crossroads and continue ascending up the Lomnistá dolina valley, which tapers in this part. The road will carry you to the **Asmolovova chata** cottage (1,00 m) next to graves and bunkers from the period of the SNU. A road marked in yellow (8448) continues up the valley and it leads to the **monument of Ján Šverma**, the hero of the Slovak National Uprising who perished here during the passage over the massive mountain of Chabenec in winter. The route of the trip deviates to the green-marked forest road beyond the parking lot. The road ascends up the forest and the switchbacks run through the forest. It heads to the **Struhárske sedlo** saddle (1,355 m) situated on the ridge between the Lomnická and Jasenianska dolina valleys. The profile of the ascent is steep and it allows no rest. Only the central part of the ascent becomes milder while you advance along the contour line as far also the

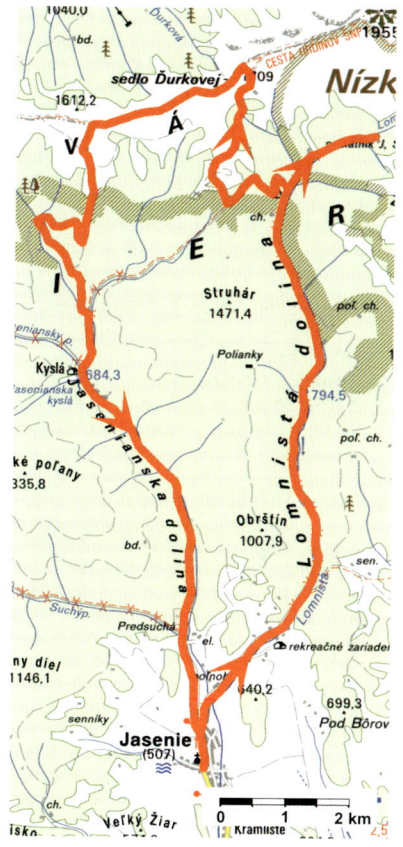

restored **shelter of Ďurková** (1,640 m) with a spring. Short rest will renew your energy needed for the short final ascent to the **crossroads** (1,730) above the saddle of **Sedlo Ďurková** (1,709 m). This is the point where you finally start to ascend to the main ridge of the Nízke Tatry Mts. The ridge trail of the Cesta hrdinov SNP marked in red (E8, 0801) is a short one heading to the west as far as the shallow saddle below the **Zámostská hoľa Mt.** (1.591 m). There is a distinct elevation of **Ďurková** (1,750 m) situated between the two saddles, the highest point of the trip. Leaving it behind continue westward and in the saddle below the Zámostská hoľa Mt. turn left onto the descending path marked in yellow (8448). Before reaching the upper timber line pass by a hut with a spring next to it. Continue descending down the grassy ridge on an old road to the spruce forest on the slope of the **Gelfusová** valley. The winding road descends down to the valley where it continues on the left side of the brook. At the point where it joins the valley of Šifrová dolina is a crossroads where you turn right onto the blue-marked trail (2639) heading to the recreation centre of **Kyslá** (684 m). Tasting the excellent mineral water from the spring **Jasenianska kyslá** there is a long though comfortable descent down the **Jasenianska dolina** valley. Next to the **gamekeeper's lodge Predsuchá** (650 m) you will pass by a small water power plant. This unique technical monument was built in 1925. A half an hour walk will bring you to the aim of the trip in the village of **Jasenie**.

7 The ridge of Skalka

Krpáčovo – Skalka – Kotliská – Vajskovská dolina – Krpáčovo

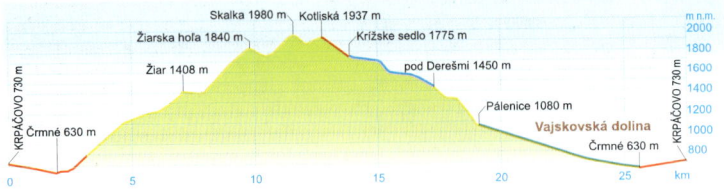

Situation: The Nízke Tatry Mts. – South (western part).
Starting and finishing point: Krpáčovo, bus stop, parking lot.
Time schedule: Krpáčovo - Črmné ½ h - Strmý vŕštek ½ h - Pálenička 1 ½ h - Žiarska hoľa 1 h - Skalka ¾ h - Kotliská ¼ h - Krížske sedlo ½ h - Pod Derešmi 1 h - Pálenice 1 h - Dve vody 1 ½ h - Črmné ½ h - Krpáčovo ½ h.
Total: 9 ½ hours.
Elevation gain: 1,350 m.
Map: Nízke Tatry - Chopok 1 : 50 000 (sheet 122), VKÚ, š. p., Harmanec.

Classification: Difficult and strenuous all-day high mountain tour with great altitude difference.
Basic route: Start at the final bus station next to the Biotika hotel in **Krpáčovo** (730 m) following the red mark (0816), which heads to the west. You will abandon the asphalt road leading on the foothills of the mountain range when you reach the monument on alpine meadow **Črmné** (630 m) in the lower part of the Vajskovská dolina valley. Beyond the crossroads with the green-marked trail the cart road leads to the bridge over the Vajskovský potok brook and continues further to the west. The yellow-marked path (8447) to be followed as far as the end of the ascent to the main ridge of the Nízke Tatry Mts. joins the red mark next to the bridge. Continue from the head of the dolina Borové valley ascending in steeper slope to **Strmý vŕštek** (809 m). Turn left at the crossroads onto the forest road ascending up the forested ridge to the alpine meadow of **Pálenička** (1,120 m). The ascent is fairly demanding. It continues as far as the shallow saddle bellow **Žiar** (1,300 m). A steep step leads from the saddle to the rocky mountain of **Žiar** (1,408 m). Another step lies above the upper timber line and it is grown over by dwarf pine trees. The route of ascent leads from the ridge to the east. Pass by the group of rocks called Bosorky and behind them the round **Žiarska hoľa Mt.** (1,840 m) rises. The top is on the right side of the road and the view it offers is indeed wonderful. There are side ridges on both sides of the main ridge known as dangerous avalanche terrain. It was precisely here, on the south-eastern slope of the Žiarska hoľa Mt. where a terrible avalanche fell killing 16 forest workers in 1965. The last terrain step is in the highest part of the side ridge. Once you climb it you will find yourself

on the top of the ridge of **Skalka** (1,980 m), the tallest side ridge in the whole Nízke Tatry Mts. The reward comes in form of unique panoramic view of the surrounding landscape. Descend down the narrow ridge to **Kotliská** (1,937 m) eventually reaching the main ridge of the Nízke Tatry Mts. Continue to northeast to the **Krížske sedlo** saddle (1,775 m) where you turn right in the direction of the Vajskovská dolina valley. The descent follows the blue mark (2626) and it traverses the southern slope of the Dereše Mt. crosses the zone of dwarf pine forest and a series of troughs. The path shortly touches the upper timber line of spruce forest. At the crossroads (1,450 m), the point denoted on the maps as **"drevenica pod Derešmi"** (ruins of the old hut stand several meters away from it) turn right onto the abruptly descending path marked in yellow (8443) and descend to the bottom of the Vajskovská dolina valley. There is a remarkable technical work to admire on the alpine meadow of **Pálenice** (1,080 m), the chutes for floating timber down the brook restored by the employees of the National Park of the Nízke Tatry Mts. If you have enough time you should also see the **Vajskovský vodopád** waterfall. It takes about an hour to go and another to return to the basic route. The descent down the Vajskovská dolina valley on cart road is long but fairly interesting. Another detour from the basic route is possible next to the hunter's hut at **Dve vody** (710 m). You will need about one hour to visit the **monument in the Kulichova dolina** valley, which commemorates the victims of already mentioned disastrous avalanche. You will return from Dve vody comfortably to **Krpáčovo** passing through the alpine meadow of **Črmné**.

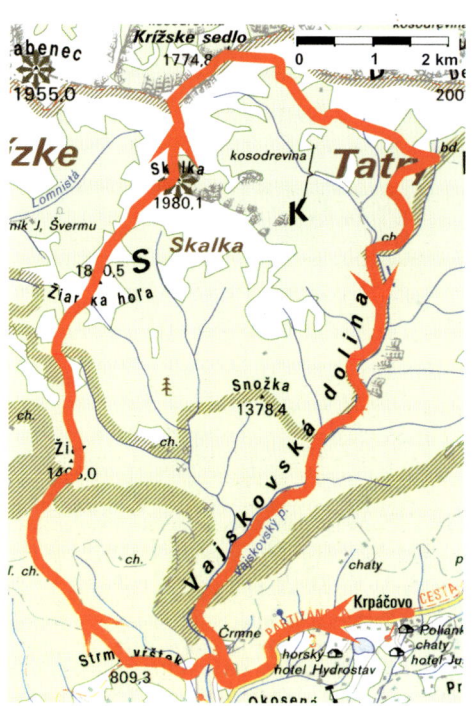

8 Around Krpáčovo and Lehoty
Krpáčovo – Horná Lehota – Dolná Lehota – Krpáčovo

Situation: The Nízke Tatry Mts. – South (western part).
Starting and finishing point: Krpáčovo, bus stop, parking lot.
Time schedule: Krpáčovo - Prameň Sama Chalupku ½ h - Horná Lehota 1 h - Dolná Lehota ¾ h - Črmné 1 h - Krpáčovo ½ h
Total: 3 ¾ hours.
Elevation gain: 250 m.
Map: Nízke Tatry - Chopok 1 : 50 000 (sheet 122), VKÚ, š. p., Harmanec.

Classification: Easy and comfortable walk on cart roads and paved paths. The stretch between the two villages of Lehota lacks hiking marks.
Basic route: Start at the recreation centre of **Krpáčovo** (730 m). Look for the yellow mark (8429) near the Junior hotel. The paths heads to the east for a short while and then it turns to the south. It runs along the Hnusné brook. Beyond Paseky near the brook is the spring **Prameň Sama Chalupku** (650 m), which bears the name of poet Samo Chalupka (1812-1883) who was born and died in the village of Horná Lehota. The route crosses the brook from the right to the left bank and continues along the stream for more than 2 km. Another bridge will carry you back to the right side of the valley where the road ascends in forested slope to end up on a plain called Lúčky. The road descends from the plain down to the valley and the village of **Horná Lehota** (640 m). You should not miss the visit to the **commemorative room of the poet Samo Chalupka** next to the church and cemetery with the grave of the famous author at the lower end of the village. Continue on the main street northward and turn to the first side lane on your left. The lane heads to the west and joins the field road, which leads to the village of **Dolná Lehota** (480 m). The road joins asphalt road at the upper end of the village. Turn right and follow the green hiking marks (5427). There are several karstic phenomena on the surrounding slopes (small caves and sinkholes). Comfortable asphalt road will carry you as far as the head of the Vajskovská dolina valley with the gamekeeper's lodge of **Črmné** (640 m). Turn right at the crossroads on alpine meadow below the gamekeeper's lodge and continue to the east on the piedmont hiking route also called

Krpáčovo

Partizánska cesta or Partisan's Road. After almost a kilometre and passing by the monument of the Slovak National Uprising the route returns back to the asphalt road leading to **Krpáčovo**.
Options: You can also make the trip in the opposite direction (total 3 ¾ of an hour) or finish it in Horná Lehota (total 1 ½ hours) or in Dolná Lehota (2 ¼ hours).

9 Around Krpáčovo and Tále

Krpáčovo – Tále – Krpáčovo

Situation: The Nízke Tatry Mts. – South (western part).
Starting and finishing point: Krpáčovo, bus stop, parking lot.
Time schedule: Krpáčovo - Veľká Riavka ¾ h - Tále ¾ h - Pod Brezinami ½ h - Prameň Sama Chalupku ¾ h - Krpáčovo ¼ h
Total: 3 hours.
Elevation gain: 180 m.
Map: Nízke Tatry - Chopok 1 : 50 000 (sheet 122), VKÚ, š. p., Harmanec

Classification: Easy and comfortable outing on cart roads and paths. The trail is marked except for the section between the recreation buildings of Krpáčovo.

Basic route: A side road starting at the Junior hotel in **Krpáčovo** (730 m) will carry you to the main road marked in red (0816) also called Partizánska cesta or Partisan's Road. Start to the east. The meandering and ascending asphalt road runs transversally through the **Veľká Riavka** valley (880 m). Beyond the valley it leads in the slope and drops to the holiday resort of **Tále** (700 m) lying in the widening part of the Bystrá dolina valley. Return from the Partizán hotel a bit back on the road turn left onto the yellow marked trail (8429). You will find this turning behind the Stupka hotel. The route leads to the west and on a path situated a bit lower and further south of Partizánska cesta road. It passes through the meadows called **Pod Brezinami**. There is only a half an hour walk from the brook of Riavka to Krpáčovo. The road marked in yellow avoids the recreation buildings of Krpáčovo passing by their eastern side. It leads to the valley of the Hnusné brook as far as the **Prameň Sama Chalupku** spring (see tour No. 8). Next to the bridge over the brook turn right onto a path which runs along a hayloft and heads to extensive meadows south of Krpáčovo. On the left side of the Červená voda valley are meadows with two ski lifts. This trip also heads to this valley. On the northern side of the valley ascend to a moderate slope and a plain with recreation buildings of Hydrostav and Krpáčovo water reservoir. The Junior hotel, the aim of the trip, stands east of the water reservoir.

Options: The walk can be shortened or extended using the different hiking paths and roads.

Tále

10 The Baba Mt.

Trangoška – Kosodrevina – Príslop – Pálenica – Baba – Tále

Situation: The Nízke Tatry Mts. – South (western part).
Starting point: Trangoška, bus stop, parking lot.
Cieľový bod: Tále, bus stop, parking lot.
Time schedule: Trangoška - Srdiečko ¼ h - Kosodrevina ¾ h - Príslop ½ h - Pálenica ½ h - Baba ½ h - Mesiačik ½ h - Tále 1 ¼ h
Total: 4 ¼ hours.
Elevation gain: 934 m.
Map: Nízke Tatry - Chopok 1 : 50 000 (sheet 122), VKÚ, š. p., Harmanec.

Classification: Easy and comfortable half-day trip in high-mountain environment with prevalence of dropping terrain. Pay attention to hiking marks at the section between Príslopy and Baba, as they are rather poorly discernible in the dwarf pine forest.

Basic route: Start at the parking lot at **Trangoška** (1,120 m). Asphalt road leads to now decaying **Srdiečko** hotel (1,216 m) next to the lower station of the chair lift to the Chopok Mt. Follow the yellow-marked trail (8430) and ascend from Srdiečko on switchbacks on the slope on the right side of the ski track. At about the middle of the ascent the path traverses the ski track to its left side and continues ascending to the abandoned mountain hotel of **Kosodrevina** (1,500 m) Continue along the contour line on the road towards west sticking to the yellow and blue (2626) hiking marks. The yellow trail turns off in the direction of the Chopok Mt. after about more than a half kilometre walk. Continue on the blue-marked trail. The road passing through dwarf pine forest still sticks to the contour line for about a kilometre and half. It leads to the crossroads at the **Príslop** saddle (1,518 m). Turn left there onto the yellow-marked path (8429). The ascent is mild at the beginning. It avoids the Príslop Mt. (1,557 m) and traverses to the right towards a distinct cliff and continues on a side ridge through dwarf pine forest ascending to the **Pálenica Mt.** (1,654 m). The attractive passage on the lateral ridge with wonderful views of the deep valleys on its sides starts there. The ridge maintains the altitude above sea level more or less 1,600 m. If you want to ascend to the top cliff of the **Baba Mt.** you have to turn off the path, which is avoiding it. The view of the Nízke Tatry

The Ďumbier Mt. and Kosodrevina hotel

Mts. from the top is indeed worth the toil. Also the alpine meadow at the end of the horizontal part of the side ridge lying south of the Baba Mt. offers fine views. The path copying the gradient line is rather worn out. It turns to the south and slightly descending it passes by the forehead of the massive Baba. It will carry you to the forested rocky ridge of **Mesiačik** (1,362 m) with limited views of the Bystrá dolina valley. The following part of the descent runs in spruce forest onto an old steep forest road on the eastern slope of the Veľká Riavka valley. The descent ends near the Partizán hotel in **Tále** (720 m).
Options: The basic tour is more demanding if walked in the opposite direction (total 5 hours).

11 The Ďumbier and Chopok Mts. from Trangoška

Trangoška – Chata gen. M. R. Štefánika – Ďumbier – Chopok – Kosodrevina – Trangoška

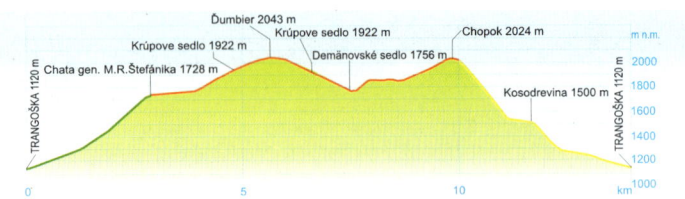

Situation: The Nízke Tatry Mts. – South (western part).
Starting and finishing point: Trangoška, bus stop, parking lot.
Time schedule: Trangoška - Halašova jama ¾ h - Chata gen. M. R. Štefánika ¾ h - Krúpove sedlo ½ h - Krúpova hoľa ½ h - Ďumbier ½ h - Krúpova hoľa ¼ h - Demänovské sedlo ¾ h - Chopok 1 ¼ h - Kosodrevina 1 ½ h - Srdiečko ½ h - Trangoška ¼ h. **Total:** 7 ½ hours.
Elevation gain: 923 m.
Map: Nízke Tatry - Chopok 1 : 50 000 (sheet 122), VKÚ, š. p., Harmanec.

Classification: Moderately difficult and demanding all-day high-mountain tour. The ascent to the Ďumbier Mt. is almost thousand meter long. The tour can be even tougher in bad weather. High-mountain tourist cottages provide shelter and refreshment if you are caught by bad weather.

Basic route: Start at the parking lot in **Trangoška** (1,120 m) and ascend up the valley of Trangoška following the green hiking mark (5426). Passing by the information centre enter the old forest road, which leads along the Bystrianka brook. It becomes steeper at the point where a sheep farm, referred to as "lower" used to stand. The path ascends in spruce forest to the former "upper" sheep farm. Passing above it you will reach the head of the valley with thick dwarf pine forest. The water at the **Halašova jama** (1,450 m) gets lost in underground. It means you have entered karstic territory. In the side trough on the southern side of the valley is the entrance to the well-known cave called **Jaskyňa mŕtvych netopierov**. The final part of the ascent leads up on debris and well-trodden stony path. The path traverses to the sharp little crest of the Veľký Gápeľ. The **Chata gen. M. R. Štefánika** cottage (1,728 m) is within sight. After relaxing at the cottage start to the north-west on a moderate-

ly ascending hiking road, which runs on the southern slope of the Ďumbier Mt. Leaving the crossroads Na Krúpovom sedle (1,760 m) there is red, blue and green marking. The blue-marked trail turns left at the saddle. An oblique traverse heads to the **Krúpova hoľa Mt.** (1,927 m). Turn right at the crossroads onto the path ascending up the ridge to the top of the **Ďumbier Mt.** (2,043 m). The tallest mountain of the Nízke Tatry Mts. will have wonderful panoramic views

The Ďumbier Mt.

for you if the weather is good. Leaving the top of the Ďumbier Mt. go back to the **Krúpova hoľa Mt.** (1,927 m) following the same trail. Continue on the most visited section of the ridge tour (in opposite direction comparing to route No. 47) marked in red (E8, 0801). Descend first to the wide grassy **Demänovské sedlo** saddle (1,756 m). Continue traversing the southern slopes of the Konské and Široká Mts. and ascend to the **Kamenná chata** cottage below the top of the **Chopok Mt.** (2,024 m). The cliff of the taller eastern top offers fine panoramic view comparable to that from the top of the Ďumbier Mt. Leave the ridge trail and continue the descent following the yellow mark (8430), which heads to the south. The trodden path abruptly descends in alternating grassy and debris-covered slope. It avoids large boulders and cuts through the dwarf pine growth. If the visibility is not perfect pay attention to the marking painted on the stones. The path arrives at the station of the chair lift to the Chopok Mt. on a road coinciding with contour line of the slope. When you reach the crossroads turn left. Blue and yellow hiking marks will carry you soon to the **Kosodrevina** hotel (1,500 m). Continue from the building of now closed hotel on the yellow-marked path on the east side of the lift track. The path leads first on the right edge of the ski track than it passes to the switchbacks running left from it. Next to the lower station of the chair lift at **Srdiečko** (1,216 m) pass onto the asphalt road, which leads to the aim of the tour, **Trangoška.**

Options: Basic tour can be shortened leaving out the ascent to the Ďumbier and Chopok Mts. Standing at the crossroads Na Krúpove sedlo turn onto the blue-marked traverse leading to Kosodrevina (total 3 ½ hours). You can use the chair lift to descend from Kosodrevina to Srdiečko. The basic route can be also walked in the opposite direction.

12 The Chopok and Dereše Mts. from Srdiečko

Srdiečko – Chopok – Poľana – Krížske sedlo – Príslop – Srdiečko

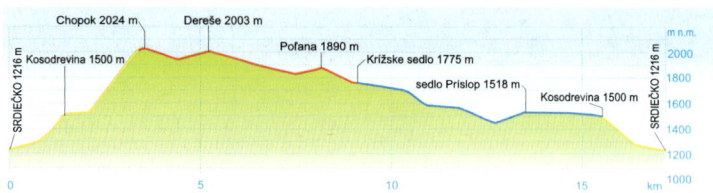

Situation: The Nízke Tatry Mts. – South (western part).
Starting and finishing point: Srdiečko, bus stop, parking lot.
Time schedule: Srdiečko - Kosodrevina ¾ h - Chopok 2 h - Dereše ½ h - Sedlo Poľana ¾ h - Poľana ¼ h - Krížske sedlo ½ h - Pod Derešmi ¾ h - Príslop ½ h - Kosodrevina ¾ h - Srdiečko ½ h.
Total: 7 ¼ hours. **Elevation gain:** 808 m.
Map: Nízke Tatry - Chopok 1 : 50 000 (sheet 122), VKÚ, š. p., Harmanec.

Classification: Moderately difficult high-mountain tour running mostly above the upper timber line. The longish section of the trip in the western part of the main ridge does not provide possibilities of refreshment or shelter in emergency.

Basic route: The ascent to the Chopok Mt. starts at **Srdiečko** (1,216 m) following the route of the final stretch of the route No. 11 in the opposite direction. After the comparatively strenuous ascent to the top of the **Chopok Mt.** (2,024 m) and a short rest on its eastern top with beautiful view and refreshment available at the Kamenná chata cottage, start on the ridge trail westward following the red marking (E8, 0801). The route includes also the stretch between the Chopok Mt. and Poľana. Steep rock faces are turned to the head of the Demänovská dolina valley. On the southern side long and high slopes covered by heaps of blocks and debris, which incline to the Bystrá and Vajskovská dolina valleys, can be seen. Descend from the Chopok Mt. first to a shallow saddle beyond which the path ascends to the slope of the **Dereše Mt.** (2,003 m). If you want to ascend to its top you have to abandon the path. After a short

The Dereše and Chabenec Mts.

descent from the Dereše Mt. a long comfortable stretch of ridge trail follows . Moderately descending you will get to the **Sedlo Poľana** saddle (1,837 m). The route of the usual descent from the ridge to the Vrbické pleso lake in the Demänovská dolina valley turns right. But your trail continues ascending on a wide ridge to the top of the Poľana Mt. (1,890 m). Do not take the yellow-marked path, which leads to the side ridge of Bôr, descend rather via ridge to the **Krížske sedlo** saddle (1,775 m), which is nearby. It is here where you leave the main ridge of the mountain range turning left and heading to the long traverse of its southern hillside. The path is moderately descending though not as much as to loose the height above the bottom of the deep glacier valley of the Vajskovská dolina valley. It gradually cuts a series of troughs, it wears through the dwarf pine stands and crosses wide denuded hilltops. The path descends below the upper timber line when passing under the Dereše Mt. If it is not windy you can hear the Vajskovské vodopády waterfalls roar. You are gradually passing by the crossroads with the yellow-marked trail and an old hut and arriving at the **Príslop** saddle (1,518 m). The road running along the contour line at the lower part of the continuos dwarf pine canopy on the southern slope of the Chopok Mt. will bring you to the **Kosodrevina** hotel (1,500 m). The way to get to **Srdiečko** is the same as in the conclusion of the tour No. 11.

13 The Ďumbier Mt. from Mýto pod Ďumbierom

Mýto pod Ďumbierom – Chata gen. M. R. Štefánika – Ďumbier – Trangoška

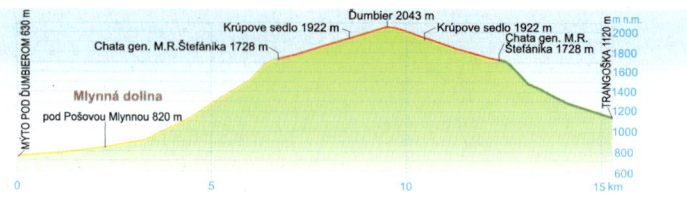

Situation: The Nízke Tatry Mts. – South (western part).
Starting point: Mýto pod Ďumbierom, bus stop, parking lot.
Finishing point: Trangoška, bus stop, parking lot.
Time schedule: Mýto pod Ďumbierom - Pod Pošovou Mlynnou 1 ¼ h - Chata gen. M. R. Štefánika 2 ¾ h - Krúpove sedlo ½ h - Krúpova hoľa ½ h - Ďumbier ¾ h - Krúpova hoľa ½ h - Krúpove sedlo ½ h - Chata gen. M. R. Štefánika ½ h - Halašova jama ½ h - Trangoška ¾ h.
Total: 8 ½ hours. **Elevation gain:** 1,388 m.
Map: Nízke Tatry - Chopok 1 : 50 000 (sheet 122), VKÚ, š. p., Harmanec.

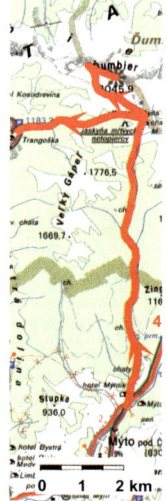

Classification: Difficult and strenuous all-day high-mountain tour with extreme altitude difference and length. It is not recommended for the short-day seasons. Possibilities of refreshment and emergency shelter is at the Chata gen. M. R. Štefánika cottage.
Basic route: Start next to the Mýto hotel, north of the village of **Mýto pod Ďumbierom** (630 m). Following the yellow hiking mark (8428) turn off the main road onto a side cart road, which heads to the **Mlynná dolina** valley. The profile of the road is mild and comfortable. The route heads left to the Zelenská Mlynná once you reach the branching of the valley next to the **Pod Pošovou Mlynnou** crossroads (820 m). It starts to ascend in the tapered part of the valley. It rises as far as the upper timber line and advances in stony trough, which becomes wet at the head of the valley. The path palliates the ascent in the very steep basin-like end of the valley by switchbacks. They will carry you to the rocky crest of the side ridge of the Veľký Gápeľ, several tens of meters away from the **Chata gen. M. R. Štefánika** cottage (1,728 m). The proper ascent from the cottage to the top of the **Ďumbier Mt.** (2,043 m) coincides with that described in the route

Mýto pod Dumbierom

No. 11. After returning from the top of the tallest mountain of the Nizke Tatry Mts. to the **Krúpova hoľa Mt**. (1,927 m) do not continue on the ridge. Return by the same way to the **Chata gen. M. R. Štefánika** cottage (1,728 m). Finish the tour descending from the cottage to **Trangoška** (1,120 m) following the route of the initial stretch of the tour No. 11 in the opposite direction.
Options: The basic route can also be walked in the opposite direction (total 8 hours).

14 The Králička Mt.

Čertovica – Králička – Starobocianska dolina – Vyšná Boca

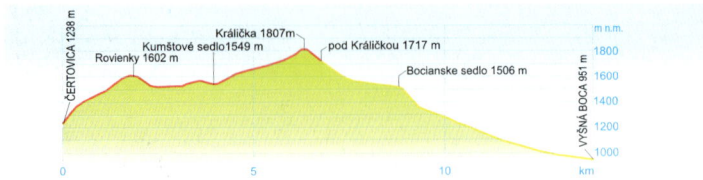

Situation: The Nízke Tatry Mts. – North (western part).
Starting point: Čertovica, bus stop, parking lot.
Finishing point: Vyšná Boca, bus stop, parking lot.
Time schedule: Čertovica - Rovienky 1 h - Kumštové sedlo ½ h - Panská hoľa ¼ h - Králička ½ h - under the Králička ¼ h - Bocianske sedlo ½ h - Pod Starou Bocou 1 h - Vyšná Boca ¼ h.
Total: 4 ¼ hours.
Elevation gain: 856 m.
Map: Nízke Tatry - Kráľova hoľa 1 : 50 000 (sheet 123), VKÚ, š. p., Harmanec.

Classification: Moderately difficult half-day, high-mountain tour.
Basic route: Start at the chata **Čertovica** cottage, which stands directly in the eponymous saddle (1,238 m) and walk on easternmost stretch of the ridge trail of the Ďumbierske Tatry Mts. Red-marked trail (E8, 0801) starts by an ascent in steep slope straight above the saddle and continues on a milder stretch of the ridge. Shortly after you will come out of the forest to a steep denuded part of the ridge called **Lajštroch** with nice view of the Kráľovohoľské Tatry Mts. Lajštroch ends at the western part by a little distinct elevation of **Rovienky** (1,602 m). Then there is the first short descent beyond Rovienky to a shallow saddle. The path forces its way through the thick dwarf pine growth. When you reach the straight stretch before arriving at the **Kumštové sedlo** saddle (1,549 m) you will get out on grassy slopes. The path crosses with the green hiking mark (5619) at the saddle. The trail still continues on the main ridge. A long ascent to the **Panská hoľa** (1,635) follows. The next top within the ridge is taller but the path avoids it. After ascending to the **Králič-**

The Čertovica saddle

ka Mt. (1,807 m) you will get a wonderful view of the mountain group of Ďumbier and the adjacent Jánska dolina valley. Then you will descend to the crossroads in the shallow hollow under the **Králička** (1,717 m). Turn right onto the yellow marked path (8428). Go down the slope along the remains of the past mining activities and short switchbacks will carry you to the Jánska dolina valley. The path does not descend as low as the bottom of the valley, it turns to the slightly descending traverse at the middle of the slope. The oblique path will lead you to the grassy **Bocianske sedlo** saddle (1,506 m). The path crosses again the green-marked trail, which ascends to the Rovná hoľa Mt. However, your route leads from the saddle like tour No. 27 to the village of Vyšná Boca. Descend to the Starobocianska dolina valley. In the upper part of the stretch walk down the switchbacks of an old mining road and somewhat lower you will ascend to moderately descending cart road. Walking along the Boca brook you will descend as far as the **Pod Starou Bocou** crossroads. You will get to the **Vyšná Boca** (951 m) sticking to the frequented main road.

15 The Beňuška Mt.
Čertovica – Beňuška – Braväcovo

Situation: The Nízke Tatry Mts. – South (eastern part).
Starting point: Čertovica, bus stop, parking lot.
Finishing point: Braväcovo, bus stop, parking lot.
Time schedule: Čertovica - Sedlo za Lenivou ¾ h - Lenivá ¼ h - Beňuška ¼ h - Bukovinka ½ h - Skala ¼ h - Hlboká ¾ h - Braväcovo ¼ h.
Total: 3 hours.
Elevation gain: 926 m.
Map: Nízke Tatry - Kráľova hoľa 1 : 50 000 (sheet 123), VKÚ, š. p., Harmanec.

Classification: Moderately difficult half-day high-mountain tour with prevailing descents. Orientation is easy apart from the environs of Bukovinka

The view of the ridge near Nižná Boca

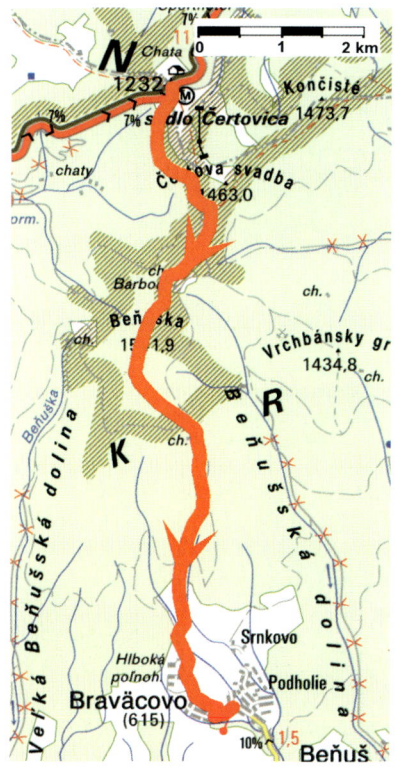

where the path cuts across several roads, which can be confusing.

Basic route: Start at the bus stop at the sedlo **Čertovica** saddle (1,238 m) going south-eastward following the red mark (E8, 0801). The road moderately ascends in the western slope of the Čertova svadba Mt. above the deep head of the Široká dolina valley. At the **Sedlo za Lenivou** saddle (1,378 m) the route leaves the Cesta hrdinov SNP road (in red) and turns right onto the green-marked trail (5424). After a while the hiking path comes out of the forest to the **Lenivá** alpine meadow (1,434 m) with several paths on the left side. It enters again the forest at the southern edge of the alpine meadow and moderately ascends to the top meadow of the **Beňuška Mt.** (1,542 m). The highest point of the side ridge offers panoramic view of the near and distant landscape. One can even spot the Kremnické vrchy Mts., Poľana Mt., Slovenské Rudohorie Mts., and Tatras in good weather. The **Kečka Mt.** (1,529 m) provides the last wide and far-reaching views. Later you will ascend into forest. The descending route leads across clearings with the hut at **Bukovinka** (1,300 m). Passing by a massive rock tower called **Skala** (1,170 m) it is about half-way of your descent from the Beňuška Mt. to the village of Braväcovo. The path comes out of the forest above the Hlboká brook in the eponymous valley. It disappears from time to time but the view of the village is a reliable point of orientation. Before entering the village you will pass by the gamekeeper's lodge of **Hlboká** (680 m). If there is not convenient bus connection in **Braväcovo** continue following the green mark to Beňuš, which lies on the main road and it also has railway station.

16 From Bacúch to Vyšná Boca

Bacúch – Bacúšske sedlo – Vyšná Boca

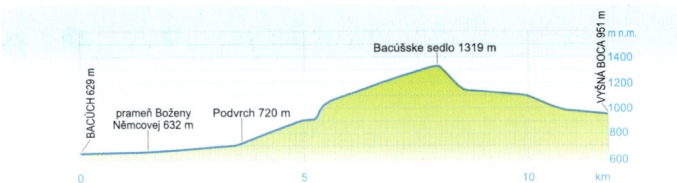

Situation: The Nízke Tatry Mts. – South (eastern part).
Starting point: Bacúch, bus stop, railway station, parking lot.
Finishing point: Vyšná Boca, bus stop, parking lot.
Time schedule: Bacúch - Prameň Boženy Němcovej ¾ h - Podvrch ½ h - Bacúšske sedlo 2 h - Vyšná Boca 1 h
Total: 4 ¼ hours.
Elevation gain: 690 m.
Map: Nízke Tatry - Kráľova hoľa 1 : 50 000 (sheet 123), VKÚ, š. p., Harmanec.

Vyšná Boca

Classification: Moderately difficult half-day route with prevailing ascents in forest landscape. Orientation is easy. Pay attention at the crossroads of forest roads.

Basic route: Start at the railway station of **Bacúch** (629 m) following the blue mark (2613), which goes through the village. On the right of the valley beyond the village is the **Prameň Boženy Němcovej** spring (632 m) bearing the name of the known Czech lady-writer who once visited the local spa. After having a gulp of its exquisite mineral water you will be fit to ascend up the Bacússka dolina valley. Leaving the spring return to the forest asphalt road, which will carry you to the cottage situated at the place where the valley branches, called Podvrch (720 m). Reaching the **Podvrch** leave the road and continue on switchbacks of stony path

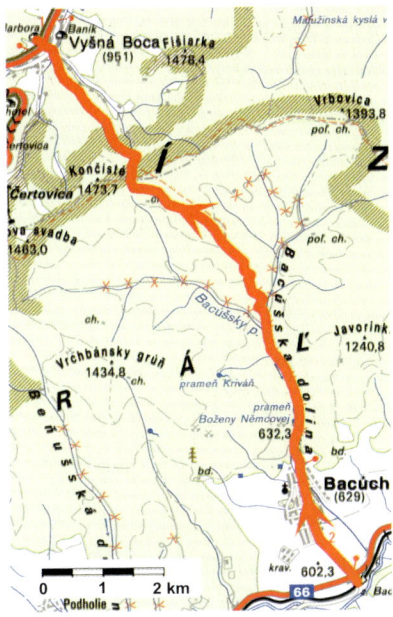

ascending up the forested Jánov grúň Mt. Its lower part leads along the main Bacússka dolina valley later it passes to the Adamova dolina valley. The highest point of the route is the **Bacússke sedlo** saddle (1,319 m). Once you pass the shallow saddle at the main ridge, all there is left is descent. Follow the blue hiking mark as far as Vyšná Boca. The path heads to the left side of the Podvrch valley. Continue from the saddle to the left on moderately descending traverse along the brook. The switchbacks of the path descend through the forest to an open trough. After a while turn left onto a dug out path and descend on the hillside of the Salvátor Mt. Cross the wide draining channel and continue across the forest above the village of Vyšná Boca. Continue among the log houses onto asphalt road. Turn first to the right, then to the left and you will find yourself at the bus stop in the village of **Vyšná Boca** (951 m). If you want to arrive at the upper stop on the road from Čertovica you will have to go up through the village to the church, turn right up the path running along the cemetery, cross the tunnel under the road and go up the stairs to the Barbora hotel (next to the church across the brook is a shelter with fine mineral water spring).

17 The Homôľka Mt.

Polomka – Homôľka – Oravcová – Závadka nad Hronom

Situation: The Nízke Tatry Mts. – South (eastern part).
Starting point: Polomka, bus stop, railway station, parking lot.
Finishing point: Závadka nad Hronom, bus stop, railway station, parking lot.
Time schedule: Polomka - Ždiarska dolina ½ h - Bukovinka ¾ h - Salašná ¾ h - Homôľka saddle ½ h - Homôľka ¼ h - Homôľka saddle ¼ h - Zadná hoľa ¼ h - Pod Oravcovou ¾ h - Krivý most ½ h - Kolesárová ¾ h - Závadka nad Hronom 1 h. **Total:** 6 ½ hours.
Elevation gain: 1,033 m.
Map: Nízke Tatry - Kráľova hoľa 1 : 50 000 (sheet 123), VKÚ, š. p., Harmanec.

Classification: Moderately difficult high-mountain tour with large altitude difference. Orientation is comparatively easy apart from the upper stretch of the descent from the Pod Oravcovou crossroads.
Basic route: The trip starts at the railway station in **Polomka** (628 m) and it leads through the village following the green-marked trail. It heads to the end of the **Ždiarska dolina** valley. At the crossroads (740 m) at the lower part of the valley turn onto its eastern slope. Steep path in the forest quickly reaches the ridge of the **Bukovinka Mt.** and continues ascending to the southern piedmont of the Homôľka Mt. The alpine meadow of **Salašná** (1,415 m) offers the view of the surrounding mountains and the ridge of the Nízke Tatry Mts. The path ascends from Salašná (1,415) following the gradient line as far as an old stony road heading to the shallow **Homôľka** saddle (1,570 m) on the main ridge of the mountain range. On the slope of the dolina Rakyťanka valley is a little hut commemorating the events, which took place here by the end of 1944 when the Nazi troops took prisoners the soldiers of English and American mission, which where here to help the local partisan groups operating around Homôľka. There is also a tablet at the saddle commemorating the events. West of the saddle is the cone-shaped **Homôľka Mt.** (1,600 m). Red-marked trail (E8, 0801) ascends its slope. The top is not on the route but the view of the southern slope of this mountain is captivating. It includes the deep furrow of the Heľpianske podolie valley, wide massif of the Fabova hoľa Mt. and more mountains of the forested Slovenské rudohorie mountain range. After returning back to the saddle of

Homôľka use the Cesta hrdinov SNP road to advance eastward. Walking in dwarf pine forest you will easily reach the **Zadná hoľa Mt.** (1,619 m) with the massive side ridge of Veľký bok turned to the north. There is also the yellow-marked (8626) hiking trail but you will stick to the red-marked path heading to the forested **Oravcová Mt.** (1,544 m) within the main ridge. The hiking path also avoids this top. At the **Pod Oravcovou** crossroads (1,460 m) turn right onto the blue mark (2627). The route of descent is initially moderate but it becomes steeper next to the Krivý most Mt. (1,215 m). It leaves the ridge inclined to the south at the Dlhý grúň turning to the left to the dolina Úplaz valley. The descent in the wide draining channel on the right side of the valley will easily carry you to the crossroads at the gamekeeper's lodge of **Kolesárová** (745 m). At the point where the dolina Úplaz valley contacts the Stratenská dolina valley stands the gamekeeper's lodge. You can see the buildings of the Sigma recreation centre on the opposite slope of the dolina Úplaz valley. Going in the opposite direction on the asphalt road, which leads to them you will arrive at the aim of the trip, the village of **Závadka nad Hronom** (627 m). The railway station lies in the lower part of the village next to the river Hron.

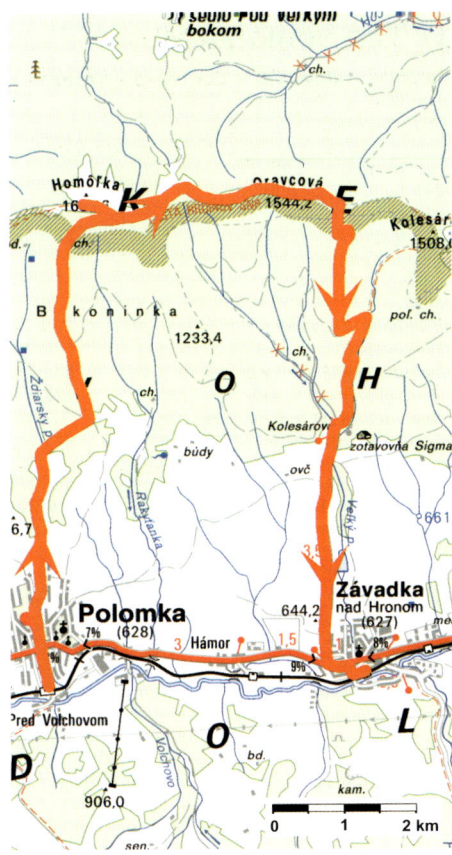

18 The Veľká Vápenica Mt.

Heľpa – Priehyba – Veľká Vápenica – Priehybka – Heľpa

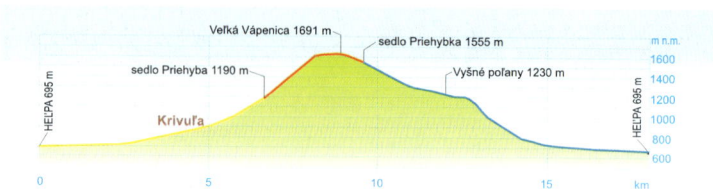

Situation: The Nízke Tatry Mts. – South (eastern part).
Starting and finishing point: Heľpa, bus stop, railway station, parking lot.
Time schedule: Heľpa - Heľpa-rázcestie ¾ h - Priehyba 1 ½ h - Veľká Vápenica 1 ½ h - Priehybka ¼ h - Vyšné poľany ½ h - Heľpa 2 h. **Total:** 6 ¼ hours.
Elevation gain: 996 m.
Map: Nízke Tatry - Kráľova hoľa 1 : 50 000 (sheet 123), VKÚ, š. p., Harmanec.

Classification: Moderately difficult high-mountain tour with comparatively large altitude difference.

Basic route: Start at the railway station of **Heľpa** (695 m) situated at the western edge of the village, continue to the centre following the main road. Yellow and blue are the hiking marks of your route. Turn left at the centre of the village onto the road heading to the upper end of the village below the Holý vrch Mt. There is the crossroads (730 m) beyond the village. Do not turn right onto the blue mark. Stick to the asphalt road ascending to the **Krivuľa** valley. The route is marked in yellow (8421) and heads to the sedlo Priehyba saddle. If you stayed on the asphalt road the ascent would be easier but also longer. Fortunately there is a shortcut marked in yellow. Turn onto it before you reach the first wide bend in the upper part of the valley. The old road you are ascending on up the forest crosses once more the asphalt road and then it ascends to the **Priehyba** saddle (1,190 m) almost following the gradient line. This saddle is the second lowest situated place of the main ridge of the Nízke Tatry Mts. Steep forest road ascends to it and it is part of the

The Veľká Vápenica Mt.

Cesta hrdinov SNP road (E8, 0801). The ascent is strenuous. The road changes into path, which will carry you to the **Veľká Vápnica Mt.** (1,691 m). The terrain requires increased attention in order to spot the red marks. When the path reaches the upper timber line it winds between rocks and dwarf pine trees while it ascends to the top with wonderful panoramic view. The descent from the Veľká Vápenica Mt. to the **Priehybka** saddle (1,555 m) is much shorter and quicker than that to the Priehyba saddle, which is situated almost 400 m lower. The ridge trail crosses the hiking path connecting the villages Heľpa and Čierny Váh at the saddle. Choose its southern branch at the crossroads turning to the right. The descent on the blue mark (2716) heads above the head of the dolina Koleso valley to the forested ridge of the Chotárny grúň Mt. The trail descends down the forested **Vyšné poľany Mt**. (1,230 m). Then it becomes steep again next to the cliff called Organy. The final stretch runs in grassy landscape as far as the **crossroads** above the village. At the crossroads (730 m) choose the same asphalt road, which you used before to ascent to the sedlo Priehyba saddle. The road will carry you comfortably to the aim of the trip in **Heľpa**.

19 The Andrejcová Mt.

Pohorelá – Andrejcová – Ždiarske sedlo – Pohorelá

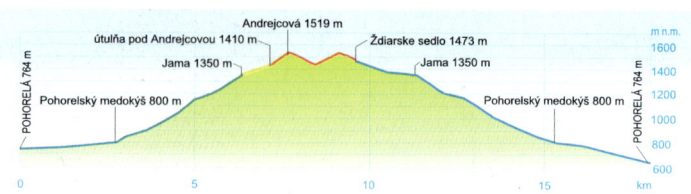

Situation: The Nízke Tatry Mts. – South (eastern part).
Starting and finishing point: Pohorelá, bus stop, railway station, parking lot.
Time schedule: Pohorelá - Pohorelský medokýš ¾ h - Jama 1 ¾ h - shelter below Andrejcová ½ h - Andrejcová ¼ h - Ždiarske sedlo ½ h - Jama ¾ h - Pohorelá 2 h.
Total: 6 ½ hours.
Elevation gain: 755 m.
Map: Nízke Tatry - Kráľova hoľa 1 : 50 000 (sheet 123), VKÚ, š. p., Harmanec.

Classification: Moderately difficult high-mountain tour with comparatively large altitude difference. The shelter below the Andrejcová Mt. provides for emergency cases if the weather deteriorates.

Basic route: Cross the village of **Pohorelá** (764 m) from the railway station as far as the upper end of the villages. Follow the blue hiking marks (2621). The maintained path next to the last village houses will carry you to the **Pohorelský medokýš spring** (800 m). After testing this agreeable mineral water continue up the steep ridge of the Úplazik Mt. on the southern hillside of the Andrejcová Mt. In its lower part the trail leads on the pastures and in its upper part is runs on abandoned forest road, which enters the spruce forest. There is crossroads on the forest clearing called **Jama** (1,350 m). Turn left onto the yellow mark (8420) The road incised in the slope heads to a small alpine meadow on the main ridge, which offers beautiful views of the valley of Heľpa. On the northern edge of the forest is the **shelter below Andrejcová** (1,410 m). Next to it is the spring called Zimná voda. The path continues from the shelter on the main ridge of the Nízke Tatry Mts. Follow the red hiking mark (E8, 0801) passing the main ridge to Ždiarske sedlo saddle. The moderate ascent ends at the round top of the

The shelter below the Andrejcová Mt.

Andrejcová Mt. (1,519 m) with fine views. The profile of the ridge trail continues dropping into the shallow **Ždiarske sedlo** saddle (1,473 m). Near the saddle on the southern side is a spring. Blue hiking mark (2848) turns left from the saddle, heads to the Ždiarska dolina valley and further to Liptovská Teplička. However, you will continue in the opposite direction on stony path, which is also marked in blue (2621). The landscape around you quickly changes and spruce forest substitutes the dwarf pine growths. The trail slightly descends down the steep slope of the dolina Pod Úplazom valley to the clearing of **Jama** (1,350 m) where it meets the trail you have used to ascend to the Andrejcová shelter. Use the trail to descend to **Pohorelá** passing by the spring again.

20 The Kráľova hoľa Mt. from Telgárt

Telgárt – Kráľova hoľa – Šumiac

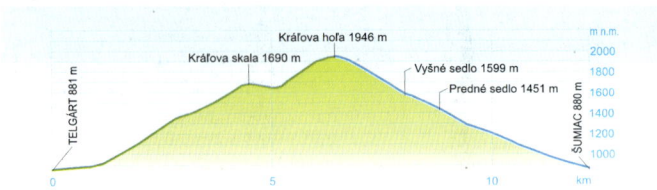

Situation: The Nízke Tatry Mts. – South (eastern part).
Starting point: Telgárt, bus stop, railway station, parking lot.
Finishing point: Šumiac, bus stop, parking lot.
Time schedule: Telgárt - Kráľova skala 2 ½ h - Snehová jama ½ h - Kráľova hoľa ¾ h - Vyšné sedlo ½ h - Predné sedlo ¼ h - Šumiac 1 ¼ h. **Total:** 5 ¾ hours.
Elevation gain: 1,066 m.
Map: Nízke Tatry - Kráľova hoľa 1 : 50 000 (sheet 123), VKÚ, š. p., Harmanec.

Classification: Moderately difficult high-mountain tour with comparatively large altitude difference. In case of poor visibility you can use the longer route going down asphalt road, which ends in the village of Šumiac. The buildings at the top of the Kráľova hoľa Mt. are not open to public. The Mountain Rescue Service has its station installed in the building of the TV transmitter.

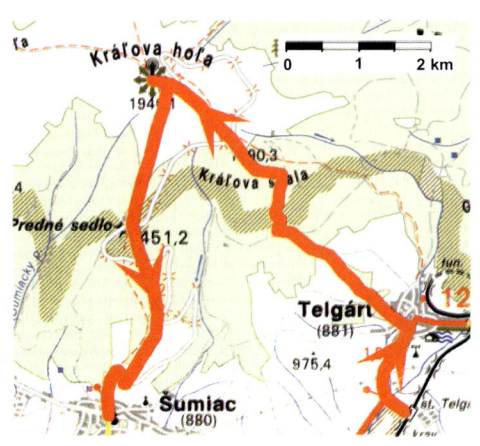

Basic route: Start at the railway station in **Telgárt** (881 m) and continue to the centre of the village. At the crossroads next to the municipal office continue further on the road in the direction of Brezno and then turn left onto the street heading to the church. Follow the green hiking marks (5439). Reaching the edge of the village continue up amidst pastures with rests of forest and young growths on the south-eastern slope of the Kráľova skala rock. After the short stretch on a path, which copies the contour line, the ascent becomes steeper. Short switchbacks will carry you soon above the tallest spruce trees and to the belt of dwarf pine growth. Now you are not far from the top of the **Kráľova skala Mt.** (1,690 m). From the top of this schist rock you can see the next reaches of the route leading to the top of the massive Kráľova hoľa Mt. (1,946 m). Descend down the debris slope to the **Snehová jama** saddle

The view from the Kráľova hoľa Mt.

(1,650 m). In the shallow depression also called Kráľovo sedlo the asphalt road coming from Šumiac and heading to the TV tower on top of the Kráľova hoľa Mt. crosses your route. If you choose this road to continue to the top, the trip will result more comfortable but also longer. If you stay on shorter and steeper trail, continue on hardly discernible path marked in green, which will bring you in less than an hour to the top rocks of the **Kráľova hoľa Mt.** (1,946 m). You will eventually make use of a short stretch of the asphalt road while approaching the top. If you want to enjoy the much appraised panoramic views you should better climb up the rocks at the top. The view of the Tatras is indeed unforgettable. Descend choosing the shortest and steepest option of descent following the blue-marked hiking trail (2610). The path follows the gradient line on the southern slope of the massive mountain. Below the **Vyšné sedlo** saddle (1,599 m) it becomes steeper and descends to the **Predné sedlo** saddle (1,451 m). Orientation was easy so far as the track of the ski lift ran parallel to the path. The trail crosses with the asphalt road to Šumiac at the Predné sedlo saddle. It will meet with it another three times before you enter the village. It is better to use the road if the path is wet and muddy. But if it is dry you will reach **Šumiac** (880 m) far sooner.

Options: The mountain range can be also crossed if you continue from the top of the Kráľova hoľa Mt. following the green mark heading to the north (route No. 21) and descend to the Liptovská Teplička (total 7 ¼ hours). You can also go back to Telgárt following the red mark (total 6 ¼ hours). The tour can be also walked in opposite direction. It offers a very steep and quick access to the top (total 5 ½ hours).

21 The Kráľova hoľa Mt. from Liptovská Teplička

Liptovská Teplička – Kráľova hoľa – Orlová – Liptovská Teplička

Situation: The Nízke Tatry Mts. – North (eastern part).
Starting and finishing point: Liptovská Teplička, bus stop, parking lot.
Time schedule: Liptovská Teplička - Veľký Brunov 1 ¾ h - Záturňa 1 h - Čierny Váh-prameň 1 ¼ h - Kráľova hoľa ¾ h - Orlová 1 ¼ h - Ždiarske sedlo ¾ h - Stanikovo 1 h - Ždiar ¾ h - Liptovská Teplička 1 ¼ h. **Total:** 9 ¾ hours.
Elevation gain: 1,027 m.
Map: Nízke Tatry - Kráľova hoľa 1 : 50 000 (sheet 123), VKÚ, š. p., Harmanec.

Classification: Moderately difficult high-mountain tour with comparatively long and strenuous ascent to the Kráľova hoľa Mt. The fact that the mountain is so massive and wide is the cause why there is relatively long distance between the top and the surrounding settlements. In case of bad weather you can quickly return to Šumiac using the asphalt road, which was built as access road to the TV tower at the top of the mountain.

Basic route: Start at the typical mountain village of **Liptovská Teplička** (919 m). The green-marked hiking trail leads in picturesque landscape consisting of varied mosaics of narrow fields, meadows and pastures arranged in terraces. The torrent of Čierny Váh will accompany you as far as the **Veľký Brunov** gamekeeper's lodge. You will abandon the valley of this mountain group, which becomes the longest Slovak river, by turning to the side valley of Veľký Brunov. After about one and a half kilometre walk you will also abandon this picturesque valley and ascend on winding path to the **Záturňa** saddle (1,213 m) under the eponymous mountain. Passing through beautiful alpine meadow you will enter spruce forest again and it will last as far as the **Lapinová** alpine meadow in the upper part of the little valley Malý Brunov. The ascent then enters the dwarf pine belt. The spring of the Čierny Váh deserves a short stop on the path ascending in oblique traverse of the northern hillside of the Kráľova hoľa Mt. At this place you will realize why this mountain is also called the "roof of Slovakia". Apart from the Čierny Váh also other important Slovak streams, the Hron, Hornád, and Hnilec, spring on the slope of this massive mountain. The view from the top of the **Kráľova hoľa Mt.** (1,946 m) adorned by bizarre rocks corresponds to the fact that this dominant mountain at the middle of Slovakia is visible from near and distant places. You can see the Muránska planina plateau and Stolické vrchy Mts. in the south, karstic plateaux of the Slovenský raj Mts. in the east, and the main ridge of the Nízke Tatry Mts. in the east. But the north boasts the most beautiful horizon: the Vysoké Tatry and Západné Tatry Mts. towering high above the sub Tatra basins. The following stretch of the trip is the passage over the most beautiful and highest part of the eastern ridge of the Nízke Tatry Mts. Leaving the Kráľova hoľa Mt. behind

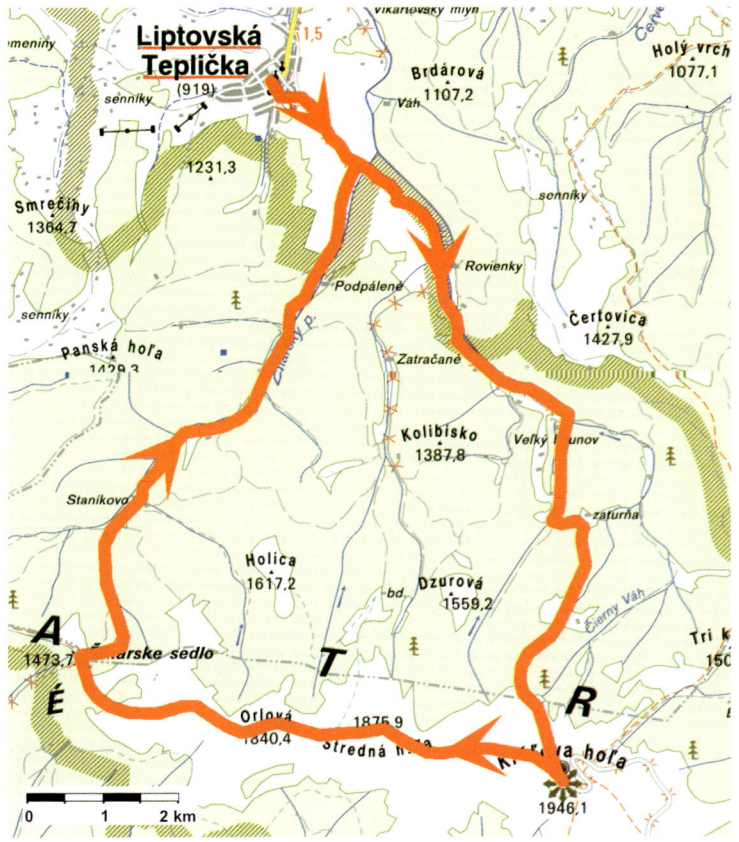

start to the west on the lightly dropping **Cesta hrdinov SNP** road marked in red (E8, 0801). The path gradually overcomes the three round hills of the Stredná hoľa Mt. (1,876 m), Orlová Mt. (1,840 m), and Bartková Mt. (1,790 m) covered by alpine meadows and large debris fields. Reaching the **Ždiarske sedlo** saddle (1,473) turn right and start the comparatively long descent to the Liptovská Teplička on the blue-marked trail (2848). The path descending from the saddle soon enters the spruce forest and the switchbacks drop to one of the branches of the **Ždiarska dolina** valley. It comes to the main valley passing through a large alpine meadow above the **Staníkovo** gamekeeper's lodge (1,100 m). Comfortable road running down the valley will carry you to the Výpad crossroads (907) where it communi-

The top of the Kráľova hoľa Mt.

cates with your route. Now you reach the road you used to ascend to the Kráľová hoľa Mt. in the morning. You will easily reach the aim of the trip, **Liptovská Teplička.** Unusual tiny earth hills you see around are the traditional cellars where the locals keep potatoes.

Options: The three alternative descents from the Kráľova hoľa Mt. are oriented to the south, the Horehronie region. The most beautiful *Option A* descends on the blue-marked trail (like tour No. 20) almost following the gradient line) and ends in the village of Šumiac (6 ¾ hours). *Option B* concludes the trip by descent on the green-marked trail to Telgárt (total 7 ½ hours). The aim of the *Option C* is the same. It uses the Cesta hrdinov SNP, red-marked trail, for descent (total 7 hours).

The massif of the Kráľova hoľa Mt.

22 Around Liptovská Teplička

Liptovská Teplička – Doštianka – Liptovská Teplička

Situation: The Nízke Tatry Mts. – North (eastern part).
Starting and finishing point: Liptovská Teplička, bus stop, parking lot.
Time schedule: Liptovská Teplička - Kufajka ¼ h - Poldvorné ¼ h - Doštianka ¾ h - Liptovská Teplička 1 h.
Total: 2 ¼ hours.
Elevation gain: 345 m.
Map: Nízke Tatry - Kráľova hoľa 1 : 50 000 (sheet 123), VKÚ, š. p., Harmanec.

Classification: Easy walk on field roads around the village suitable for any type of hikers. Open landscape with views reduces the risk of going astray.
Basic route: Start at the centre of village of **Liptovská Teplička** (919 m). Advance down the village on main road (northward) to the part called **Kufajka** (890 m). Turn onto the only street on the left and continue westward on field road leading on the bottom of a shallow valley. The road passes by haylofts on the alpine meadows of **Poldvorné**. It ascends the plain pastures at the head of the valley. The majority of the numerous haylofts, which used to stand here are now in decay. Stick to the road heading to the west and slightly ascending to the little denuded round hill of **Doštianka** (1,235). The view of the Tatras in fine weather is fantastic from its top. Continue in the picturesque landscape of the Teplická dolina valley. Return back to the crossroads next to the remaining haylofts. Turn right onto the field road, which will

Liptovská Teplička

carry you to a cross. Passing by the cross turn left onto the road, which heads to the east. You do not have to stick to the field roads. The walk on green pastures is also very comfortable and pleasant. Descend the moderate slope to get to the road at the valley of Teplička. There is forest on your left and ski lifts on your right. The road will carry you to the south-western end of the village **Liptovská Teplička** and its centre is not far away.

Liptovská Teplička

23 The Kozí kameň Mt.

Lučivná – Lopušná dolina – Kozí kameň – Vikartovce

Situation: The Kozie chrbty Mts.
Starting point: Lučivná, bus stop, railway station, parking lot.
Finishing point: Vikartovce, bus stop, parking lot.
Time schedule: Lučivná - Table ¾ h - Lopušná dolina ¼ h - Tabličky 1 h - Kozí kameň ½ h - Tabličky ½ h - Jakubčáková ½ h - Vikartovce ¾ h.
Total: 4 ¼ hours.
Elevation gain: 585 m.
Map: Nízke Tatry - Kráľova hoľa 1 : 50 000 (sheet 123), VKÚ, š. p., Harmanec.

Classification: Easy half-day trip on good roads and paths, with easy orientation. Ascents are moderate and easy.
Basic route: The tour starts at the railway station of **Lučivná** (670 m). It follows the yellow hiking mark (8747) through the village and continues southward to the fields on moderate slope. It leads in shallow depression, passes by spruce forest. The top of the grassy hill of **Table** (886 m) above ski lifts offers one of many wonderful views of the Vysoké Tatry Mts. Passing through the spruce forest you will arrive at the cottage settlement in the **Lopušná dolina** valley (770 m). Turn to south-east following the green mark (5731), which ascends to the valley of Kúty. The valley branches beyond the ski centre with ski lift on the right side next to the Štefánikova gamekeeper's lodge. The route runs in its right branch as far as to the saddle of **Tabličky** (1,060 m). The blue-marked path (2834) leads from the saddle to the top of the **Kozí kameň Mt.** (1,255 m). The northern edge of the top platform offers

the most beautiful view of the Vysoké Tatry Mts. The path running through the forest will easily carry you to the alpine meadow of **Jakubčáková** (970 m). The yellow-marked trail (8747) coming from the Malá Lopušná dolina also leads there. The basic route sticks to the green mark and heads to the south. The path descends and leaves the forest. This is the place from which you can spot the aim of the trip, the village of **Vikartovce** (756 m).

Options: The ascent to the Kozí kameň Mt. is possible from three salient points: Spišská Teplica (3 ½ hours), Vikartovce (2 hours to the top), and from Svit (2 ½ hours). The tour can be also walked in opposite direction (total 4 ¼ hours).

The panorama of the Tatras from Lučivná

24 The Veľký bok Mt.

Svarín – Svarínska dolina – Veľký bok – Hodruša – Malužiná

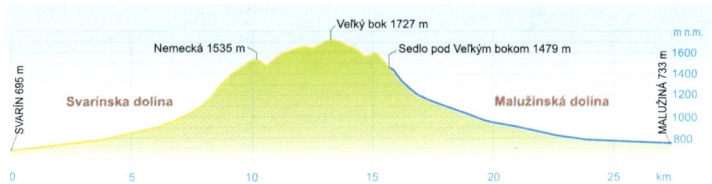

Situation: The Nízke Tatry Mts. – North (eastern part).
Starting point: Svarín, parking lot.
Finishing point: Malužiná, bus stop, parking lot.
Time schedule: Svarín - Nemecká 2 ½ h - Veľký bok 1 h - Sedlo pod Veľkým bokom ½ h - Hodruša ½ hod - Škarkétka ¾ h - Predné ¾ h - Malužiná 1 ¼ h.
Total: 7 ¼ hours.
Elevation gain: 1,032 m.
Map: Nízke Tatry - Kráľova hoľa 1 : 50 000 (sheet 123), VKÚ, š. p., Harmanec.

Classification: Moderately difficult high-mountain tour running in partially forested mountain landscape comparatively far from the settlements.
Basic route: Start at the village of **Svarín** (695 m) at the bending of the road leading to Čierny Váh turning to the left and following the yellow mark (8626) southward. Comfortable asphalt road leads up the rocky Varínska dolina valley, which tapers in places into bizarre gorge. The trail becomes steeper along the stretch starting next to the forest hut called Katka and the valley branches near the next hut. The trail heads to the Torysa valley, which has steep troughs in its head dividing the slope between the Nemecká and Veľký bok Mts. The marking carries on up the left trough and steep forested slope as far as the contour line path, which heads to a shallow little saddle on the ridge left from the Nemecká Mt. The route continues from the saddle to the right onto the ridge and carries you as far as the top of the **Nemecká Mt.** (1,535 m). The hiking path rather avoids the top. It almost disappears on the ridge and the direction of the ascent is indicated by marks painted on stones. You will get to the wide top of the Veľký bok Mt. (1,727 m) walking on the right edge of the high situated karstic plain. The trail returns to the karstic plain from the top of the Veľký bok Mt. that offers panoramic view of the surrounding landscape. This time it sticks to its other (western) edge. The route of the descent leads to the south and drops to the thin forest on stony road, which will carry you to the **Sedlo pod Veľkým bokom** saddle (1,478 m). There used to stand a tourist cottage burnt down by the Nazi soldiers in 1994 in this place. A tablet commemorates the events

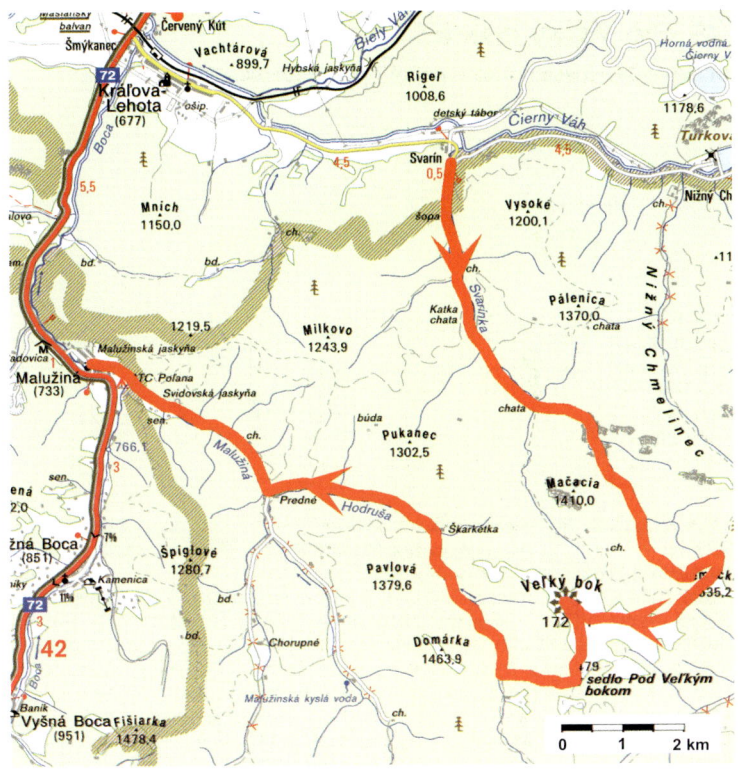

that took place there by the end of the 2nd World War. Abandon the yellow mark at the shallow saddle. A comparatively unpleasant descent on switchbacks of an old mining road towards the brook flowing at the bottom of the valley follows. It is marked in blue (2715). The profile of the route changes from the gamekeeper's lodge at **Hodruša** (1,195 m) to a long but in fact comfortable descent on cart road down the valley of **Hodruša**. Next to the gamekeeper's lodge of **Predné** (810 m) the Hodruša valley contacts the large **Malužinská dolina** valley. Asphalt road running down this valley will carry you to the final point of the trip, the village of **Malužiná** (733 m). The fine view of the picturesque landscape with beautiful rock silhouette of the Hradište Mt. will make the end of the trip even more pleasant.

25 The Rovná hoľa Mt.
Nižná Boca – Črchľa – Rovná hoľa – Bocianske sedlo – Vyšná Boca

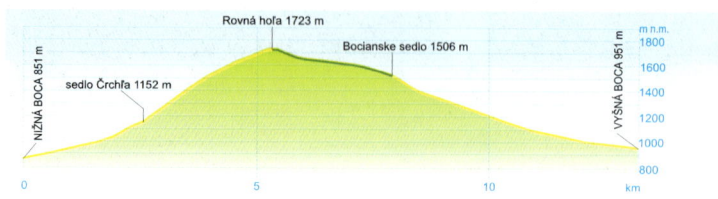

Situation: The Nízke Tatry Mts. – North (western part).
Starting point: Nižná Boca, bus stop, parking lot.
Finishing point: Vyšná Boca, bus stop, parking lot.
Time schedule: Nižná Boca - Črchľa 1 h - Rovná hoľa 1 ½ h - Bocianske sedlo 1 h - Pod Starou Bocou 1 h - Vyšná Boca ¼ h.
Total: 4 ¾ hours.
Elevation gain: 872 m.
Map: Nízke Tatry - Kráľova hoľa 1 : 50 000 (sheet 123), VKÚ, š. p., Harmanec.

Classification: Moderately difficult high-mountain half-day tour. The first stretch is steep and slippery if wet. Orientation at the top part becomes a problem if the visibility deteriorates.
Basic route: Start at the bus stop on the road, which runs around the village **Nižná Boca** (851 m) following the yellow hiking mark (8627). The route of ascent follows the road up the grassy valley. Turn onto the path ascending in the head of the bowl-like valley and continue as far as the **Črchľa** saddle (1,152 m). The saddle offers fine view of the rock galleries next to the Ohnište Mt. Turn left at the saddle onto forested steep north-eastern ridge of the **Rovná hoľa Mt**. (1,723 m). As you draw closer to small cliff you will ascend above the upper timber line. Continue passing through thick dwarf pine forest as far as the plain. Turning left traverse it and you will reach the more moderate south-eastern ridge of the Rovná hoľa Mt. Dwarf pine trees accompany you even at the top of the Rovná hoľa Mt. (1,722 m). But they do not hinder beautiful panoramic views of the

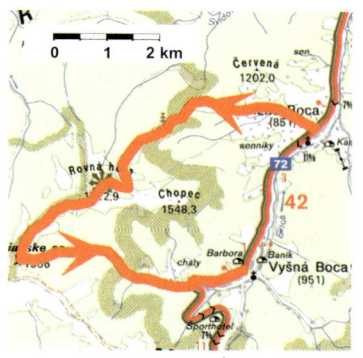

The Rovná hoľa Mt.

environs. Descend going to the south-west following the green mark (5619). The route leads along the ridge on its southern part alternatively in dwarf pine growths and grassy clearings. Traces of the past mining activity are discernible here. Then the path runs down the ridge. This stretch provides beautiful views of the Jánska dolina valley and the group of mountains around the Ďumbier Mt. Turn left onto the yellow marked trail (8428) at the wide grassy saddle of **Bocianske sedlo** (1,506 m). Descend to the valley of the Starobocianska dolina. The upper stretch of this descent runs on switchbacks of an old mining road. Once you reach the basin-shaped alpine meadow, ascend to cart road. The descent continues along the brook of Boca as far as the crossroads of **Pod Starou Bocou**. The final stretch to the village of **Vyšná Boca** (951 m) runs along the frequented main road.

Options: *Option A* deviates at the top of the Rovná hoľa at the saddle to the right branch of the path marked in green. It turns right at the Svidovské sedlo saddle and crossing the dolina Svidovo valley it ends in Malužiná (total 5 ½ hours). *Option B* leads from the Bocianske sedlo saddle across the Kumštové sedlo saddle to Čertovica (total 4 ½ hours).

26 Instructive path around the river Váh

Liptovský Ján – Liptovská Porúbka

Situation: The Nízke Tatry Mts. – North (western part), Liptovská kotlina basin.
Starting point: Liptovský Ján, bus stop, parking lot.
Finishing point: Liptovská Porúbka, bus stop, parking lot.
Time schedule: Liptovský Ján - Kaštieľske lazy ½ h - Váh ½ h - Hrádocký most 1 h - Liptovská Porúbka ½ h.
Total: 2 ½ hours.
Elevation gain: 36 m.
Map: Nízke Tatry - Kráľova hoľa 1 : 50 000 (sheet 123), VKÚ, š. p., Harmanec.

Classification: Easy and undemanding walk with minimum altitude difference, which follows the instructive trail. Beware of the falling stones along the stretch next to the place where the Belá river mouths into the Váh.
Basic route: The route of **the instructive path** starts next to the spring at the upper end of the village of **Liptovský Ján** (634 m). It has six stops with boards bearing commentaries to the adjacent areas of caves and the rafting activity once carried out on the Váh. The route of the instructive path first avoids the forested protuberance of the ridge of the Kameničná mountain, it leads along its foothill line. Opposite the Sankt Johann hotel it turns to the south-east. Less than a kilometre beyond the ski track near **Kaštieľske lazy** (670 m) the route draws closer to the channel of the Váh river, where it runs along the spring of excellent mineral water. The instructive path runs up the stream copying its meanders. The car camping site of Borová Sihoť can be seen on the other bank of the river. Following the next meander is the **Hrá-**

docký most bridge where you can abandon the route of instructive path and end the trip in Liptovský hrádok on the right bank of the river. The instructive path continues from the bridge along the red-marked hiking trail. After about a half kilometre it diverges from the river channel of the Váh and heads to the aim of the trip, the village of **Liptovská Porúbka** (650 m).
Options: You can shorten the basic route by turning off at the Hrádocký most over the Váh river to Liptovský hrádok (total 2 hours).

The swimming pool in Liptovský Ján

27 The Ohnište Mt.

Liptovský Ján – Jánska dolina – Ohnište – Slemä – Stanišovská dolina – Liptovský Ján

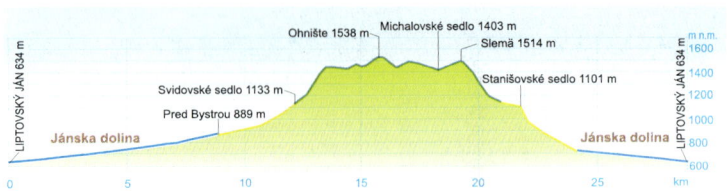

Situation: The Nízke Tatry Mts. – North (western part).
Starting and finishing point: Liptovský Ján, bus stop, parking lot.
Time schedule: Liptovský Ján - end of Stanišovská dolina 1 h - Pred Bystrou 1 ¼ h - Svidovské sedlo 1 ¼ h - Ohnište 1 ½ h - Michalovské sedlo ¾ h - Slemä ¾ h - Stanišovské sedlo 1 h - end of Stanišovská dolina ¾ h - Liptovský Ján 1 h.
Total: 9 ¼ hours.
Elevation gain: 904 m.
Map: Nízke Tatry - Chopok, Nízke Tatry - Kráľova hoľa 1 : 50 000 (sheet 122, 123), VKÚ, š. p., Harmanec.

Classification: Difficult and strenuous all-day tour mostly on well prepared paths and roads, which does not ascend to the high-mountain environment above the upper timber line. It is demanding for its length. The long stretch in the Jánska dolina valley runs on comfortable asphalt road.
Basic route: The tour starts in the formerly famous yeoman village of **Liptovský Ján** (634 m). If you resist the opportunity to stay at the local thermal swimming pool continue on asphalt road with blue hiking marks (2626) up the **Jánska dolina** valley. After about an hour walk you will pass by the yellow-marked deviation to the Stanišovská dolina valley on the left, which you will make use of on the return trip. The constantly changing natural setting with rocks of diverse forms with sinkholes and caves makes the comfortable walk trough the valley as far as the **Pred Bystrou** gamekeeper´s lodge (889 m) more pleasant. Turn left at the gamekeeper's lodge onto the yellow-marked trail (8625) heading to the Svidovské sedlo saddle via the **Púchalka** alpine meadow (940 m). Meanwhile, you will spot for the first time the imposing rock galleries of the **Ohnište Mt.** (1,538 m) you are aiming at. You are going to ascend its top plateau from the **Svidovské sedlo** saddle (1,133 m). Ascend on steep but well-maintained path with green hiking marks (5619). The top is accessible by a short detour from the extensive plateau alpine meadow of **Ohnište**. Follow the green triangles. Not far from the top are the 125 m deep **Veľká ľadová priepasť** abyss and the 10 m high opening in the rock called **Okno** (Window). The green trail (5619) continues

from the meadow of the Ohnište to the north-west in the forest. Beyond the shallow **Michalovské sedlo** saddle (1,403 m) the switchbacks of the path ascend to the forested **Slemä Mt.** (1,514 m). The wrack of plane and the monument are the reminders of the tragic event, which took place here in the 2nd World War next to the mountain top. The path descends from the top of the Slemä to the Brtkovičná dolina valley. It passes by the reconstructed bunker from the time of the Slovak National Uprising. At the crossroad above the **Brtkovica** meadow (1,169 m) with haylofts turn left onto the yellow-marked path (8624), which ascends to the **Stanišovské sedlo** saddle (1,101 m). Continue from the crossroads at the saddle on the yellow mark and descend to the **Stanišovská dolina** valley. Cross the whole of the valley as far as the point where it contacts the Jánska dolina valley. At the **crossroads** at the head of the **Stanišovská dolina** valley (718 m) turn right onto the blue-marked trail (2626) and continue down the Jánska dolina as far as **Liptovský Ján**.

Options: *Option A* shortens the tour, instead of ascending from the Svidovské sedlo saddle to the Ohnište, descend on yellow trail to the village of Malužiná in the Bocianska dolina valley (total 4 ¼ hours). *Option B* abandons the basic route at the crossroads above the Brtkovica meadow and descends down the Brtkovičova dolina valley to the village of Liptovský Hrádok (total 8 ½ hours).

28 The Smrekovica Mt.

Liptovský Ján – Stanišovská dolina – Smrekovica – Liptovský Ján

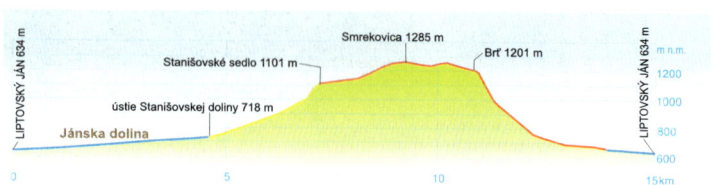

Situation: The Nízke Tatry Mts. – North (western part).
Starting and finishing point: Liptovský Ján, bus stop, parking lot.
Time schedule: Liptovský Ján - end of Stanišovská dolina 1 h - Stanišovské sedlo 1 ¼ h - Smrekovica ¾ h - Liptovský Ján 1 ½ h. **Total:** 4 ½ hours.
Elevation gain: 651 m.
Map: Nízke Tatry - Chopok, Nízke Tatry - Kráľova hoľa 1 : 50 000 (sheet 122, 123), VKÚ, š. p., Harmanec.

Classification: Moderately difficult trip on mostly well-maintained paths and roads, which does not ascend to high-mountain altitude above the upper timber line. The long stretch across the Jánska dolina valley runs on comfortable asphalt road.

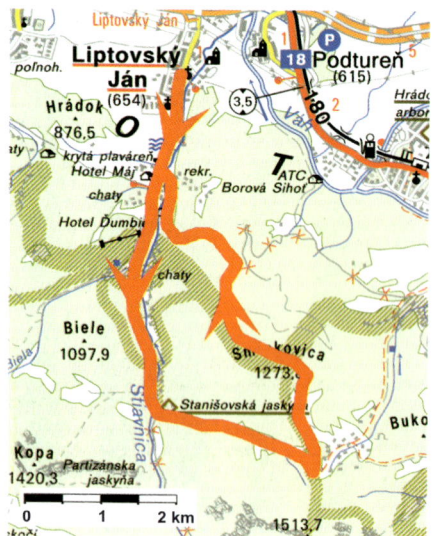

Basic route: The trip starts at the formerly famous yeoman village of **Liptovský Ján** (634 m). Comfortable asphalt road marked in blue (2626) will carry you up to the valley. Pass the crossroads below the swimming pool (655 m) with a left turning of the red-marked trail. You, however, will continue up the Jánska dolina valley, pass by the Ďumbier hotel, rehabilitation centre of Bystrá, and various recreation buildings scattered in the lower part of the picturesque **Jánska dolina** valley. Abandon the main valley at the crossroads next to the end of the **Stanišovská dolina** valley (718 m), turning left onto the yellow-marked trail (8624). Continue up the **Stanišovská dolina** valley alternatively in forest and alpine meadow to the **Stanišovské sedlo** saddle (1,101 m). The saddle is situated in agreeable meadow landscape at the head of the Brtkovičná valley. At the crossroads of the saddle turn left onto the red-marked trail (0863). Continue on the ridge. The lower part of the path runs along the edge of the meadow and forest. It enters the forest and becomes steeper. It becomes milder only at the highest part of the massive mountain of **Smrekovica** (1,285 m). The path avoids the top, it traverses the northern slope of the dominant and drops to the elevation point of **Brť** (1,201 m). The path turns right here and descends through the forest. When it reaches a

The Jánska dolina valley

small foothill plain, it turns left and runs down the side valley along the Albertovica brook. Above the cottages at the end of the valley turn left on an inclined meadow. The access road to the Marta Pension will carry you as far as the crossroads above the swimming pool. The village of **Liptovský Ján** boasts several historical and cultural monuments worth seeing.

Options: The tour can be also walked in opposite direction (total 4 ½ hours).

29 The Ďumbier Mt. from Liptovský Ján

Liptovský Ján – Jánska dolina – Chata gen. M. R. Štefánika – Ďumbier – Jánska dolina – Liptovský Ján

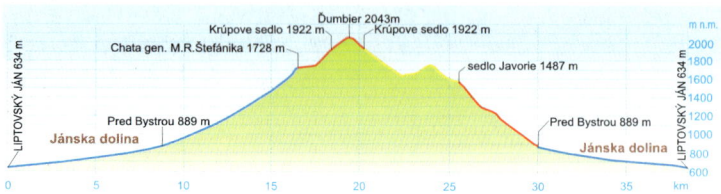

Situation: The Nízke Tatry Mts. – North (western part).
Starting and finishing point: Liptovský Ján, bus stop, parking lot.
Time schedule: Liptovský Ján - end of Stanišovská dolina 1 h - Pred Bystrou 1 ¼ h - Chata gen. M. R. Štefánika 2 ¾ h - Rázcestie na Krúpove sedlo ½ h - Krúpove sedlo ½ h - Ďumbier ¾ h - Krúpove sedlo ½ h - Prašivá ½ h - Javorie ¾ h - Pred Bystrou 1 ¼ h - end of Stanišovská dolina 1 h - Liptovský Ján 1 h. **Total:** 11 hours.
Elevation gain: 1,409 m.
Map: Nízke Tatry - Chopok 1 : 50 000 (sheet 122), VKÚ, š. p., Harmanec.

Classification: Moderately difficult all-day high-mountain tour with great altitude difference. The length of the tour predetermines it for summer months, but the long stretch of the Jánska dolina valley runs on comfortable asphalt road, which can be also walked in falling dark. The Chata gen. M. R. Štefánika cottage provide shelter and refreshment in emergency.
Basic route: The trip start at the village of **Liptovský Ján** (634 m) and the first stretch coincides with that of the tour No. 27. Comfortable ascent following the blue mark (2626) up the bizarre karstic Jánska dolina valley will carry you to the **Pred Bystrou** gamekeeper's lodge (889 m). Stick to the axis of the main valley, which is called Štiavnica, and continue on the blue-marked trail. The road sticks to the left bank of the brook in the lower part of the valley. It changes into the path passing trough the clearings and dwarf pine forest above the hut of Brenkus. At the glacier depression between the ridge of the Ďumbier and Králičky Mts. the path ascends to a steep slope. You can have some rest and refreshment at the **Chata gen. M. R. Štefánika** cottage (1,728 m) after this long ascent. Then you will make use of a short stretch of the ridge trail marked in red (E8, 0801). Traversing path will carry you to the crossroads at the **Krúpove sedlo** saddle (1,922 m). Short steep detour from the crossroads leads to the top of the **Ďumbier Mt.** (2,043 m). After having enjoyed the unique view from the tallest peak of the Nízke Tatry Mts. you can return to the crossroads at the **Krúpove sedlo** saddle tracing the way of the ascent. Continue from the saddle to the north following the

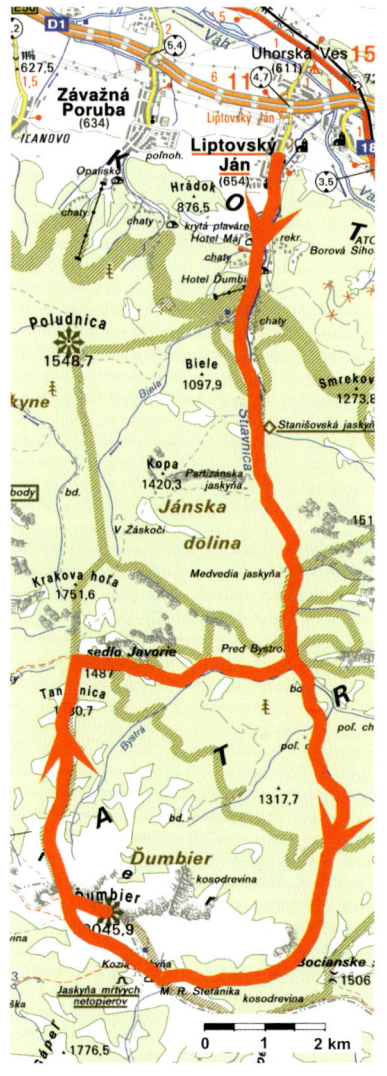

yellow mark (8620), which copies the side ridge of the Krakova hoľa Mt. Unusual views from the descending path of the split northern slopes of the Ďumbier Mt. dropping to the heads of the Bystrá and Ludárova dolina valleys are also rewarding. Do not miss the views from the scarcely discernible elevation called **Kráľov stôl** (1,775 m). The descent is rather steep at the beginning, then it becomes milder. Avoid the elevation on the side ridge of the **Prašivá Mt.** (1,667 m) and descend to the shallow saddle of **Salašky** (1,556 m). Slightly ascending path leads now to the slope of the **Tanečnica Mt.** (1,681 m). It avoids the top hidden amidst dwarf pine growth. Yellow hiking marks will carry you as far as the **Javorie** saddle (1,487 m), behind which the majestic Krakova hoľa Mt. towers. Turn right onto the red marked hiking trail (0861). Continue first on the steep forest path and cart road to the gamekeeper's lodge **Pred Bystrou** where you started the ascent in the valley of Štiavnica. Return following the familiar blue-marked trail (2626) to **Liptovský Ján**.

Options: The quickest retreat from the tour after reaching the top of the Ďumbier Mt. is the return to the Chata gen. M. R. Štefánika cottage and the descent on the green trail to Trangoška (total 10 ¼ hours).

30 The Poludnica Mt.

Iľanovo – Poludnica – Suchá dolina – Opalisko – Závažná Poruba

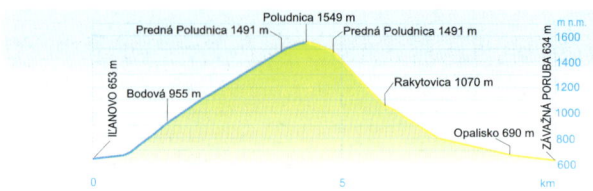

Situation: The Nízke Tatry Mts. – North (western part).
Starting point: Iľanovo, bus stop, parking lot.
Finishing point: Závažná Poruba, bus stop, parking lot.
Time schedule: Iľanovo - Bodová ¾ h - Predná Poludnica 1 ¼ h - Poludnica ¼ h - Predná Poludnica ¼ h - Rakytovica ¾ h - Opalisko ¾ h - Závažná Poruba ¼ h.
Total: 4 ¼ hours.
Elevation gain: 915 m.
Map: Nízke Tatry - Chopok 1 : 50 000 (sheet 122), VKÚ, š. p., Harmanec.

Classification: Moderately difficult half-day tour with comparatively steep ascents and descents. Easy orientation and well-discernible paths.
Basic route: The route start next to the cemetery at the upper end of the village of **Iľanovo** (653 m). Advance on the road along the farmstead and ski area to the crossroads in the **Iľanovská dolina** valley (650 m). Turn left there. Following the blue hiking marks (2709) ascend on the slope of the Vápenná (952 m). The path runs in the forest of the side valley to the alpine meadow of **Bodová** (955 m). Enter the forest again at the upper end of the

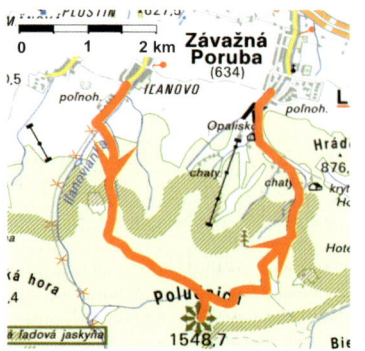

alpine meadow and continue ascending the north-western ridge of the **Predná Poludnica Mt**. (1,491 m). The natural beauty of the route is multiplied by numerous rock formations skirting the path. Switchbacks reduce steep stretches of the path and an iron ladder overcomes the steep threshold. Beautiful view of the region of Liptov from the Predná Poludnica Mt. (1,491 m) is what you get in return. If you want still more captivating view of the environs, you have to ascend further to the top of the **Poludnica Mt.** (1,549 m). The almost thousand

The ridge of the Nízke Tatry Mts. from Poludnica

meter altitude difference between the water level of the Liptovská Mara dam and the top evokes impression that you are watching the dam from a plane. You can also admire the main ridge of the Nízke Tatry Mts. with the Ďumbier Mt. After returning back to the crossroads at **Predná Poludnica** turn left onto the yellow mark (8623). The path descends down the rocky ridge as far as the alpine meadow of **Rakytovica** (1,070 m). Once you reach the crossroads at the upper edge of the alpine meadow stick to the yellow-marked path, which descends on the right edge of the meadow in the direction of the Suchá dolina valley. The descent down the steep valley will carry you to the recreation centre of **Opalisko** (690 m). Pass by the Bohunice and Tatrín hotels. In the lower part of the depression you will pass by the Opalisko cottage. The ski track seen above the cottage is one of the most difficult and feared in Slovakia. You will arrive at the village of **Závažná Poruba** (634 m) walking on slightly descending cart road.

Options: You can make the tour longer if you continue from Poludnica following the blue mark as far as the saddle below Kúpeľ. The green traverse comes back across the alpine meadow of Rakytovica to the basic route (total 6 hours).

31 The Demänovská hora Mt.

Pavčina Lehota – Demänovská hora – Iľanovské sedlo – Demänovská dolina – Pavčina Lehota

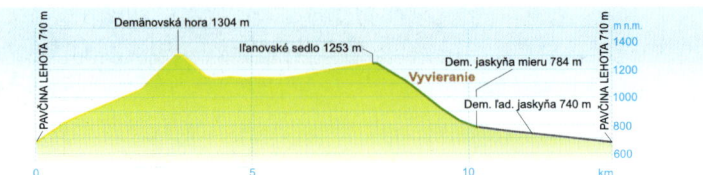

Situation: The Nízke Tatry Mts. – North (western part).
Starting and finishing point: Pavčina Lehota, bus stop, parking lot.
Time schedule: Bystrina - Pod Demänovskou horou 1 ½ h -Demänovská hora ½ h - Pod Demänovskou horou ¼ h - Iľanovské sedlo 1 ¾ h - Demänovská jaskyňa mieru ¾ h - Demänovská ľadová jaskyňa ½ h - Pavčina Lehota ¾ h.
Total: 6 hours.
Elevation gain: 614 m.
Map: Nízke Tatry - Chopok 1 : 50 000 (sheet 122), VKÚ, š. p., Harmanec.

Classification: Medium difficult tour with comparatively steep ascent and descent. It mostly runs in the forest. In the dolina Vyvieranie valley short stretches require wading in the brook especially after snow thaw or intensive rainfalls.
Basic route: Start at the bus stop next to the car camping site **Bystrina** (690 m) near the diversion to **Pavčina Lehota** (710 m). Turn right from the road leading to the car camping site onto the yellow-marked (8620) path. It winds around the forest above the camping site and hotel as far as the place in the forest where it turns right and its switchbacks ascend to a steep slope. The ascending trail keeps to the ridge between two little valleys apart from one stretch in form of large bend when it enters the valley of Smrekovica. The upper switchbacks lead to the **crossroads Pod Demänovskou horou** (1,150 m) where you have to turn onto the steep path marked by secondary marks to get to the top of the

Demänovská hora Mt.
(1,304 m). The rocky cliffs open otherwise densely forested landscape and allow nice views of the region of Liptov. Descend from the mountain also called Demänovská or Ploštínska Poludnica Mt. in older maps following the same path running in rocky relief and in forest as far as the **Pod Demänovskou horou** crossroads. Turn left at the crossroads and continue on the path following the yellow hiking mars. The path almost coincides with the contour line. You will be tra-

The Demänovská hora Mt.

versing the crest of the side ridge on its western side as far as the **Iľanovské sedlo** saddle (1,253 m). Turn right there onto the green-marked trail (5426) and descend to the picturesque valley of Vyvieranie. This karstic valley reminds of the ravines of the Slovenský raj Mts. In places you can only descend down the channel of the brook squeezed between perpendicular rocks. Climb the rock steps with what is called "the whirl pots" modelled here by the water of the brook. The bottom of the karstic valley is mostly dry but after rains or in spring snow thaw it fills with water. You have to count on wading in the cold water of the channel. The valley is closed to tourists in winter. The valley of Vyvieranie ends at the main Demänovská dolina valley next to the entrance to the **Demänovská jaskyňa mieru** cave (784 m) and to the point where the Demänovka issues and abandons the vast underground system of caves. You can get to Pavčina Lehota by the road, which runs on the right bank of the Demänovka river along the Kamenná chata (740 m) below the **Demänovská ľadová jaskyňa** cave (tour No. 32). A remarkable overhanging rock in this stretch is interesting.

Options: *Option A* diverges from the basic route at the Iľanovské sedlo saddle descending down the green trail in the Iľanovská dolina valley to Iľanovo (total 6 ½ hours). *Option B* makes the trip longer as it continues along the ridge trail marked in yellow as far as Pusté. Then you can finish the tour by descending on the blue-marked trail to the Demänovská jaskyňa slobody cave (total 5 ½ hours).

32 The Demänovská ľadová jaskyňa cave

Kamenná chata – Demänovská ľadová jaskyňa – Kamenná chata

Situation: The Nízke Tatry Mts. – North (western part).
Starting and finishing point: Demänovská ľadová jaskyňa, bus stop, parking lot.
Time schedule: Kamenná chata - Demänovská ľadová jaskyňa ½ h - Kamenná chata ½ h.
Total: 1 hour.
Elevation gain: 90 m.
Map: Nízke Tatry - Chopok 1 : 50 000 (sheet 122), VKÚ, š. p., Harmanec.

Classification: Easy and comfortable walk on well-maintained path. It is recommended to check on opening hours of the cave in advance if you want to see it.

Basic route: Next to the **Kamenná chata** cottage (740 m) at the lower part of the Demänovská dolina valley is a parking lot and bus stop of **Demänovská ľadová jaskyňa**. The trip follows the instructive trail with instructive panels, which contain information on the landmarks of the Demänovská dolina valley with special emphasis on the local valuable underground karst. The path overcomes the altitude difference of 90 m. Next to the entrance to the cave is a rock plain, which offers a unique view of the bizarre Demänovská dolina valley. The visit to the cave takes about half an hour. The return trip to the **Kamenná chata** cottage follows the same trail.

The Demänovská ľadová jaskyňa cave

The Demänovská ľadová jaskyňa cave

33 The Pusté Mt.

Demänovská jaskyňa slobody – Pusté – Vyvieranie – Demänovská jaskyňa slobody

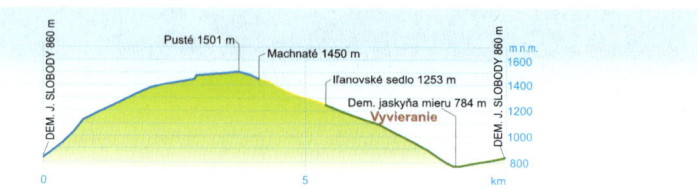

Situation: The Nízke Tatry Mts. – North (western part).
Starting and finishing point: Demänovská jaskyňa slobody, bus stop, parking lot.
Time schedule: Demänovská jaskyňa slobody - Pusté 1 ¾ h - Machnaté ¼ h - Iľanovské sedlo ½ h - Vyvieranie 1 h - Demänovská jaskyňa slobody ¼ h.
Total: 3 ¾ hours.
Elevation gain: 717 m.
Map: Nízke Tatry - Chopok 1 : 50 000 (sheet 122), VKÚ, š. p., Harmanec.

Classification: Moderately difficult half-day tour with comparatively large altitude difference including a rapid and steep ascent at the beginning. In wet weather the descent from the Iľanovské sedlo saddle to the dolina Vyvieranie valley can be a problem.
Basic route: Start at the parking lot with bus stop. Walk up wide path, which leads to the **Demänovská jaskyňa slobody** cave (860 m). You need at least 1 ½ hour of extra time to see the cave so you should better leave it for some other time. Maintained path leads from entrance to the cave up the slope of the Točište marked in blue hiking marks (2709). The ascent is in steep slope. It becomes milder when you reach the terrain plateau with an alpine meadow. Switchbacks palliate the final rock step. The following platform with alpine meadow offers the first point of relax and then there is the second steep stretch leading to the crest with higher situated alpine meadow. More switchbacks follow to the last

The Pusté Mt.

rock step. Continue traversing the steep grassy slope as far as the top of the **Pusté Mt.** (1,501 m) The plain top is also often referred to as Prašivé. Apart from fine views also the rock galleries on the southern side of the ridge are interesting. Similar rocky formations but higher situated are at the Ohnište Mt. above the Jánska dolina valley (tour No. 27). Short descent will bring you to the **Machnaté** saddle (1,450 m) in the side ridge between the Demänovská hora Mt. and Krakova hoľa Mt. Continue northward following the yellow hiking marks (8620) along the crest of the side ridge. The path traversing in the northern slope of the Pusté Mt. leads to the Iľanovské sedlo saddle (1,253 m). Continue turning left onto the green-marked path (5426). The descent down the **valley of Vyvieranie** is described in tour No. 31. with the particular that instead of turning right next to the **Demänovská jaskyňa mieru** cave (784 m) go in the opposite direction. Advance on wide comfortable road leading up the Demänovská dolina valley first on the right, and beyond the ridge on the left bank mostly in the dry channel of the Demänovka river. The channel is usually dry. The aim of the trip is at the parking lot below the **Demänovská jaskyňa slobody** cave.

34 The Krakova hoľa Mt.

Lúčky – Krakova hoľa – Pusté – Demänovská jaskyňa slobody

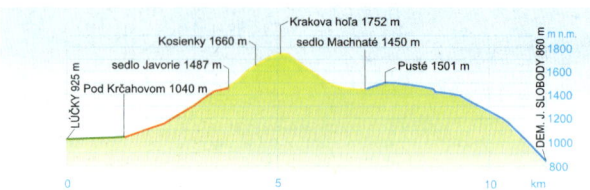

Situation: The Nízke Tatry Mts. – North (western part).
Starting point: Lúčky, bus stop, parking lot.
Finishing point: Demänovská jaskyňa slobody, bus stop, parking lot.
Time schedule: Lúčky - Pod Krčahovom ½ h - Javorie 1 h - Kosienky ¾ h - Krakova hoľa ½ h - Machnaté 1 h - Pusté ¼ h - Demänovská jaskyňa slobody ¾ h.
Total: 4 ¾ hours.
Elevation gain: 892 m.
Map: Nízke Tatry - Chopok 1 : 50 000 (sheet 122), VKÚ, š. p., Harmanec.

Classification: Moderately difficult half-day tour with comparatively large altitude difference. Poor visibility often complicates orientation. It is not recommended to abandon the hiking trail, as the rocky relief is deceptive and unpredictable.

Basic route: Start at the cottage at **Lúčky** (925 m) on slightly ascending field road, which runs on the right side of wide meadow with shrubs and trees. Follow the green hiking marks (5426). The road with stony surface ascends to the forest where there are several sinkholes on the left side. At

the **Pod Krčahovom** crossroads (1,040 m) turn left onto the red hiking trail (0861). After about 100 metres there is a turning left to the partisan bunkers in the valley of Krčahovo. If you want to see them, you have to count on about 1 hour of additional time. The red marked-trail leads on the forested slope and the path is in places hardly discernible as it advances to the alpine meadow of **Podroh** with an arbour. Continue ascending on a meadow to the dolina Podroh valley (1,175 m). There are switchbacks at the head of the valley, which lead to the saddle

The Krakova hoľa Mt. from the Pusté Mt.

of **Javorie** (1,487 m) in the side ridge between the Tanečnica and the Krakova hoľa Mt. Turn left at the saddle onto the yellow-marked trail (8620). The steep path ascends to the southern ridge of the Krakova hoľa and enters the dwarf pine forest. Then you will arrive at high situated grassy karstic plateau of Kosienka on the southern slope of the Krakova hoľa Mt. The blue-marked trail (2709) joins it from the right. The hikers use it to ascend from the Poludnica Mt. and Iľanovská dolina valley. The proper top of the **Krakova hoľa Mt.** (1,752 m) is accessible by the path, which turns right of the main yellow and blue marked path. There is a wonderful panoramic view from the top cliff of the mountain. After returning back to the crossroads continue to the right on the path, which descends down the north-western ridge. At the saddle of Machnaté sedlo (1,450 m) your trail joins the trail of the tour No. 33 though in the opposite direction. Descend over the **Pusté Mt.** (1,501 m) to the Demänovská dolina valley following the blue hiking marks. The trip ends at the parking lot below the entrance to the **Demänovská jaskyňa slobody** cave (860 m). You can see this cave, in fact one of the most beautiful Slovak caves, if you have some time left.

Option: You can return from the top of the Krakova hoľa Mt. to the alpine meadow of Kosienky and continue to the left on the blue path across the saddle of Pod Kúpeľom and Poludnica to the village of Iľanovo (total 7 ¼ hours).

35 The Siná a Bôr Mts.

Demänovská jaskyňa slobody – Siná – Bôr – Poľana – Jasná

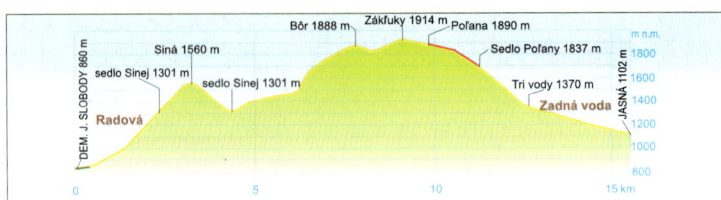

Situation: The Nízke Tatry Mts. – North (western part).
Starting point: Demänovská jaskyňa slobody, bus stop, parking lot.
Finishing point: Jasná, bus stop, parking lot.
Time schedule: Demänovská jaskyňa slobody - Pod Repiskami ¼ h - saddle of Siná 1 ½ h - Siná ¾ h - saddle of Siná ½ h - Bôr 1 h - Poľana ¾ h - Sedlo Poľana ¼ h - Tri vody 1 ¼ h - Jasná ¾ h.
Total: 7 hours.
Elevation gain: 1,030 m.
Map: Nízke Tatry - Chopok 1 : 50 000 (sheet 122), VKÚ, š. p., Harmanec.

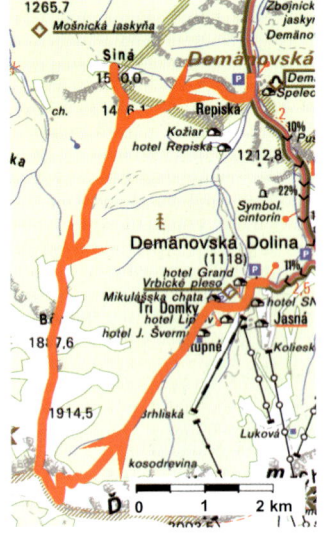

Classification: Difficult and exacting comparatively long all-day high-mountain tour with large altitude difference. Long stretch of this tour runs in high-mountain landscape above the upper timber line with unstable weather. Caution is needed in case of bad weather; it can be dangerous to abandon the trail. It is not recommended to continue from Siná on the ridge to the north-east, the terrain is difficult to climb for inexperienced hikers.

Basic route: Start at the parking lot below the **Demänovská jaskyňa slobody** cave (860 m) following the green mark (5426) to the **Pod Repiskami** crossroads (831 m) The path runs up the valley of Radová. The bottom of the picturesque valley with numerous rock formations has got short stretches in step-like channel with washed-out "whirl pots". The ascent becomes steeper once you reach the head of the valley. The path ascends in steep slope before it reaches the forested plain ridge and then continues in the forest to the saddle of **Siná** (1,301 m) in the side ridge of Bôr. Steep path leads to the right from the saddle marked in yellow secondary marks and it ends on the sharp rocky top of the **Siná Mt**. (1,560 m). The top offers a magnificent view. Do not continue further to the north, as that terrain requires mountaineering outfit and experience. Return back to the saddle of **Siná** (1,301 m) and start to ascend to the opposite slope. The long ascent on forest path will carry you to the upper

The Siná Mt.

timber line, where you enter the zone of dwarf pine forest. The profile of the tour becomes milder once you reach the next zone of denuded terrain. The high crest of the ridge offers nice views. The following moderate ascent will bring you to the top of the **Bôr Mt.** (1,888 m). If you want to get to the top of the **Poľana Mt.** (1,890 m), you will have to overcome another two elevations and three shallow saddle. The Poľana Mt. is part of the main ridge of the Nízke Tatry Mts. Turn left on the Poľana onto the Cesta hrdinov SNP marked in red hiking marks (E8, 0801). Abandon the ridge trail at the next crossroads at the **Sedlo Poľana** saddle (1,837 m). Turn left and descend down the yellow hiking mark (8619) to the Zadná voda valley. Steep ascent on ill-maintained path with switchbacks in the head of the valley follows. The path goes through the dwarf pine zone and enters forest at **Tri vody** (1,370 m). Moderate descent along the Zadná voda brook will carry you as far as the hotels below the Otupný Mt. The final stretch of the trip is on asphalt road. Left of the road is the **Mikulášska chata** cottage and **Vrbické pleso** lake (1,120 m). The tour ends at the parking lot and bus stop next to the Grand Hotel in **Jasná** (1,102 m).

36 The Demänovská and Jánska dolina valleys

Lúčky – Javorie – Jánska dolina and back

Situation: The Nízke Tatry Mts. – North (western part).
Starting and finishing point: Lúčky, bus stop, parking lot.
Time schedule: Lúčky - Pod Krčahovom ½ h - Javorie 1 h - Pred Bystrou 1 ¼ h - Púchalky ½ h - Pred Bystrou ½ h - Javorie 1 ½ h - Pod Krčahovom ¾ h - Lúčky ½ h.
Total: 6 ½ hours.
Elevation gain: 598 m.
Map: Nízke Tatry - Chopok, Nízke Tatry - Kráľova hoľa 1 : 50 000 (sheet 122, 123), VKÚ, š. p., Harmanec.

Classification: Easy tour on paths and roads of different quality including asphalt roads, which do not ascend to the high-mountain zone. Steep stretches are only around the sedlo Javorie saddle. Orientation is easy and simple.

Basic route: The initial stretch from the cottage at **Lúčky** (925 m) as far as the **Javorie** saddle (1,487 m) is the same as in tour No. 34. If you want to get a better view from the saddle go up the slope of the Krakova hoľa Mt. After this short detour continue on the red mark (0861) eastward to the Jánska dolina valley. First advance on forest path and then on cart road while you ascend to the side valley of Bočná. The red mark ends at the crossroads next to the **Pred Bystrou** gamekeeper's lodge (889 m). Continue from the gamekeeper's lodge on asphalt road heading to the south-east and follow the yellow hiking marks (8625). You do not have to ascend as far as the Svidovské sedlo saddle if you want to get fine views of the Ohnište Mt (1,538 m). The best place for it is the wide alpine meadow of **Púchalky** (940 m) and you will see the impressive rock galleries on the southern slope of this wonderful karstic mountain. Descend from Púchalky back to the gamekeeper's lodge of **Pred Bystrou** and rerun the route as far as the Javorie saddle on the return trip to **Lúčky** in the Demänovská dolina valley.

The view of the Ďumbier Mt. from the north

37 Instructive path of the Demänovská dolina valley
Jasná – Tri vody – Luková – Široká dolina – Lúčky

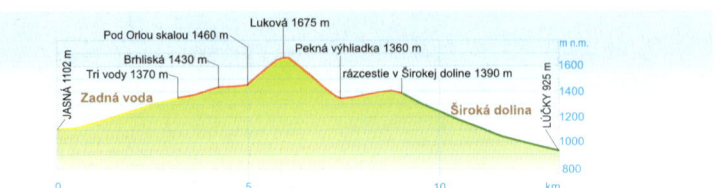

Situation: The Nízke Tatry Mts. – North (western part).
Starting point: Jasná, bus stop, parking lot.
Finishing point: Lúčky, bus stop, parking lot.
Time schedule: Jasná - Vrbické pleso ¼ h - Tri vody ¾ h - Brhliská ¼ h - Pod Orlou skalou ¼ h - Luková ¼ h - Pekná vyhliadka ¾ h - Široká dolina-rázcestie ½ h - Pod Krčahovom ¾ h - Lúčky ½ h.
Total: 4 ¼ hours. **Elevation gain:** 750 m.
Map: Nízke Tatry - Chopok 1 : 50 000 (sheet 122), VKÚ, š. p., Harmanec.

Classification: Moderately difficult half-day tour with comparatively large altitude difference. Its short stretch near Luková ascends above the upper timber line. In bad weather you can leave the tour there and quickly go down to Jasná following the blue mark.
Basic route: The whole route follows that of the **instructive path Demänovská dolina** with 12 information panels. Start at the parking lot in front of the Grand hotel east of the **Vrbické pleso** lake (1,102 m). Go round the mountain lake walking on its north-western bank as far as the Mikulášska chata cottage. Proceeding below the Otupný Mt. yellow path (8619) joins the instructive path. Ascend up the **Zadná voda valley** along the brook to the **Tri vody** crossroads (1,370 m). Turn left onto the red mark (0855). Continue on the path, which traverses the northern slope of the main ridge of the Nízke Tatry Mts. in the head of the Demänovská dolina valley. The path moderately ascends in the forested northern slope of the Dereše Mt. as far as the **Brhliská** (1,430 m),

The Vrbické pleso lake

and the funicular. Cross the ski track and when you arrive at the **Pod Orlou skalou** crossroads (1,460 m) the path starts to ascend. Its switchbacks run in dwarf pine growth towards the slope of the Chopok Mt. Beyond the last switchback starts the oblique traverse ending at the station of chair lift, now out of use, from the Otupný Mt. to **Luková** (1,675 m) and functioning chair lift from Jasná to Luková. From now on the route mostly descends. The first section of the descent leads on the slope to the station of the chair lift (1,500 m) connecting Záhradky and Konský grúň. Continue descending on the edge of the dwarf pine forest as far as **Pekná vyhliadka** (1,360 m) The profile of the tour changes. The path turns right and traverses the slope as far as the **Široká dolina** crossroads (1,390 m). The instructive path joins here the green-marked (5426) hiking trail. Yours will be the green-marked trail (5426) and it will take you along the Demänovka river down the Široká dolina valley as far as the **Pod Krčahovom** crossroads (1,040 m). The trip ends next to the cottage at **Lúčky** (925 m).
Options: The descent to Jasná can be made shorter if you chose blue-marked trail at the crossroads of Pod Orlou skalou (total 6 ½ hours). You can also leave the route at the station of chair lift and have a ride down to Záhradky. The basic route can be also walked in opposite direction (total 4 ½ hours).

38 The Chopok Mt. from Jasná
Jasná – Dereše – Chopok – Krúpova hoľa – Lúčky

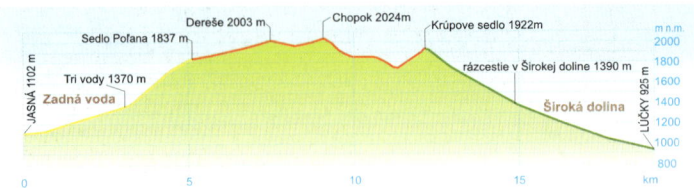

Situation: The Nízke Tatry Mts. – North (western part).
Starting and finishing point: Jasná, bus stop, parking lot.
Time schedule: Jasná - Otupné ¼ h - Tri vody ¾ h - Sedlo Poľana 1 ½ h - Dereše 1 ¼ h - Chopok ¾ h - Demänovské sedlo 1 h - Krúpova hoľa ¾ h - Široká dolina-rázcestie ¾ h - Pod Krčahovom ¾ h - Lúčky ½ h.
Total: 8 ¼ hours.
Elevation gain: 1,099 m.
Map: Nízke Tatry - Chopok 1 : 50 000 (sheet 122), VKÚ, š. p., Harmanec.

Classification: Difficult and exacting all-day high-mountain tour with large altitude difference. Only the Kamenná chata cottage below the Chopok Mt. offers emergency shelter and refreshment. Do not abandon the ridge trail.
Basic route: The first stretch of the trip coincides with the final stretch of the tour No. 35 in the opposite direction. Ascend from the parking lot in front of the Grand hotel in **Jasná** (1,102 m) up the valley of Zadná voda as far as the **Sedlo Poľana** saddle (1,837 m) You will find yourself on the main ridge of the Nízke Tatry Mts. Continue turning left on the path heading to the east, following the red hiking mark (E8, 0801). Moderate ascent leads to the **Dereše Mt.** (2,003 m) and continues over the shallow saddle to the

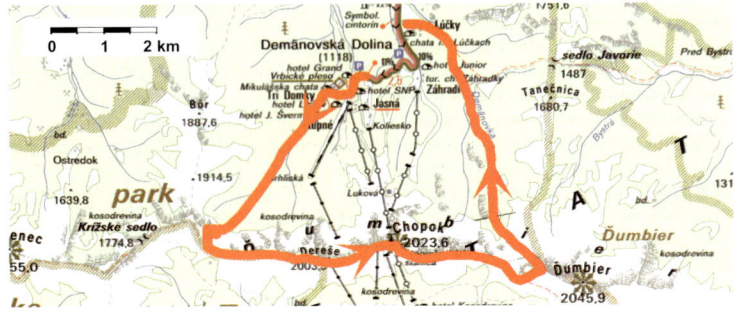

The Kamenná chata cottage below the Chopok Mt.

Chopok Mt. (2,024 m). The path avoids the Dereše Mt. The detour to the top is worth the toil if you want to have a nice view of the environs. The Kamenná chata cottage at Chopok offers refreshment and the possibility to climb to the taller eastern top of the Chopok Mt. Chair lifts on both sides of the Chopok Mt. are out of order so you should better continue on the ridge trail. The path descends to the Demänovské sedlo saddle (1,756 m). You will reach the important crossroads of hiking paths at **Krúpove sedlo** saddle (1,922 m) from the distinct depression between the couple of the best known tops of the Nízke Tatry Mts., the Chopok and Ďumbier Mts. There is a short detour to the top of the Ďumbier (2,043 m). Descend north-westward on the green-marked trail (5426). The path winds down the steep head of the Široká dolina valley (1,390 m) descending to the crossroads in the **Široká dolina** valley (1,390 m) and joins the route of the trip No. 37 there. Walking down the valley you will soon reach the cottage at **Lúčky** (925 m).

Options: *Option A* abandons the basic route at the Chopok Mt. by descent following the blue mark over Luková to Jasná (total 6 hours). *Option B* is partial shortening of the basic route. It leaves out the short ascent to the Krúpova hoľa Mt (total 7 ¼ hours) making use of the yellow-marked short-cut from the ridge of the Nízke Tatry Mts. The basic route can be also walked in opposite direction (total 8 ¾ hours).

39 The Dereše Mt. from Jasná

Jasná – Poľana – Krížske sedlo – Príslop – Dereše – Jasná

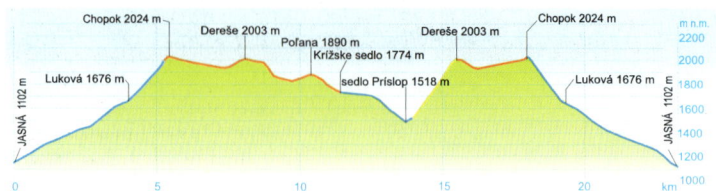

Situation: The Nízke Tatry Mts. – North (western part).
Starting and finishing point: Jasná, bus stop, parking lot.
Time schedule: Jasná - Pod Orlou skalou 1 h - Luková ¾ h - Chopok 1 h - Dereše ¾ h - Sedlo Poľana ¾ h - Poľana ¼ h - Krížske sedlo ½ h - Príslop 1 ¼ h - Dereše 1 ½ h - Chopok ¾ h - Luková ¾ h - Pod Orlou skalou 1 ½ h - Jasná ¾ h.
Total: 10 ½ hours.
Elevation gain: 922 m.
Map: Nízke Tatry - Chopok 1 : 50 000 (sheet 122), VKÚ, š: p., Harmanec.

Classification: Difficult and exacting all-day high-mountain tour with large altitude difference. The most difficult stretches in bad weather are those in the main ridge between the Dereše Mt. and Krížske sedlo saddle. In case of emergency it is better to continue from the Príslop saddle following the blue marks to Kosodrevina, or from Dereše to the Kamenná chata cottage below Chopok where you can overnight.

Basic route: Start from the Liptov hotel in **Jasná** (1,102 m) on forest path marked in blue (2079). The route of the ascent makes use of the grassy section of ski tracks. It passes under the funicular connecting the Otupné Mt. with Brhliská and ascends in forest following the gradient line to the Pod **Orlou skalou** crossroads (1,460 m). The trail joins that of the trip No. 37 and climbs to the high-mountain zone above the upper timber line. Switchbacks in dwarf pine

From the Chopok Mt. to Luková

forest will carry you to the station of chair lift at **Luková** (1,676 m). The route continues further to its final station at the **Chopok Mt.** (2,024 m). Apart from having some rest and refreshment in the Kamenná chata cottage it is also recommendable to ascend to the eastern top cliff of the Chopok Mt., which offers unusually wide view of the environs. Continue westward from the Chopok on ridge trail following the red hiking marks (E8, 0801). Now you are on the route described in trip No. 12 and continue on it as far as the **Krížske sedlo** saddle (1,775 m). You will gradually ascend to the **Dereše Mt.** (2,003 m), descend to the **Sedlo Poľana** saddle (1,837 m) and ascend to the top of the **Poľana Mt.** (1,890 m). The character of the tour changes once you leave the Krížske sedlo saddle. Continue south-eastward on a long traverse of the southern slope of the main ridge following the blue hiking marks (2626). The stretch described in tour No. 12 leads to the **Príslop saddle** (1,518 m) in the southern side ridge of the Nízke Tatry Mts. called Baba. Turn left in the saddle to the path marked in yellow (8429). The path ascends up the steep slope to the main ridge of the mountain range. Turn right at the crossroads and continue on the red mark (E8, 0801) to the **Chopok Mt.** and then turn onto the blue-marked path (2709) leading to **Luková** and **Jasná**.

40 The Predná Magura Mt.

Partizánska Ľupča – Predná Magura and back

Situation: The Nízke Tatry Mts. – North (western part).
Starting and finishing point: Partizánska Ľupča, bus stop, parking lot.
Time schedule: Partizánska Ľupča - Rumanec 1 ¼ h - Predná Magura ¾ h - Rumanec ¾ h - Partizánska Ľupča 1 h.
Total: 3 ¾ hours.
Elevation gain: 603 m.
Map: Nízke Tatry - Chopok 1 : 50 000 (sheet 122), VKÚ, š. p., Harmanec.

Classification: Easy half-day tour, with moderate altitude difference. The initial and final stretches are on asphalt road. Orientation is easy and simple as the major part of the tour follows the axis of wide ridge with open view of the environs.

Basic route: Start at the upper bus stop in the centre of the village of **Partizánska Ľupča** (568 m) going eastward on asphalt road. The whole route sticks to the yellow hiking marks (8629). When you arrive at the gamekeeper's lodge standing about a kilometre from the upper end of the village turn left onto cart road. You will abandon the road after several meters turning right onto the field road, which ascends to the northern slope of the **Rumanec Mt.** (866 m). Continue on slightly ascending grassy ridge called Mestská hora. The route copies the shape of the ridge and turns to the east. The yellow mark ends next to the top of the **Predná Magura Mt.** (1,171 m). The naked top of not very tall side ridge offers a wonderful view of the region of lower Liptov, the Chočské vrchy Mts. and Salatín Mt. You can have a look at them from another angle if you continue on the pastures on the round hillside of the ridge (outside the yellow-marked route). The tallest top of the ridge Ľupčianska Magura Mt. (1,315 m) remains hidden in the forest. Return back to **Partizánska Ľupča** (former Nemecká Ľupča) following the route of ascent.

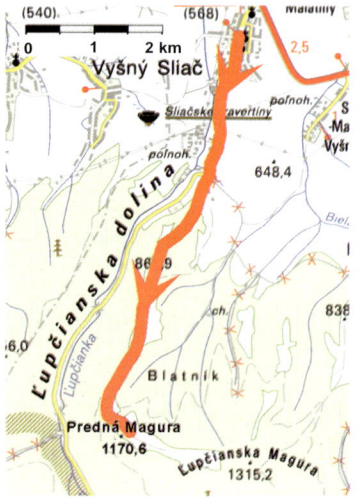

Options: The basic route can be also walked in opposite direction. The descent to Liptovské Kľačany in the north leads on unmarked paths and roads and it requires better knowing of the local terrain. The descent to the south is even more problematic and it is not recommended due to complicated orientation.

The Ľupčianska Magura Mt.

41 The travertine rocks of Sliač

Vyšný Sliač – Sliačske travertíny – Stredný Sliač

Situation: South-western part of the Liptovská kotlina basin.
Starting point: Vyšný Sliač, bus stop, parking lot.
Finishing point: Stredný Sliač, bus stop, parking lot.
Time schedule: Vyšný Sliač - Sliačske travertíny ½ h - Čertovica ¼ h - Pod Bežanom ¾ h - Stredný Sliač 1 h.
Total: 2 ½ hours.
Elevation gain: 130 m.
Map: Nízke Tatry - Chopok 1 : 50 000 (sheet 122), VKÚ, š. p., Harmanec.

Classification: Easy and comfortable walk with moderate altitude difference. It runs on unmarked paths. It is recommended on sunny days when the fascinating landscape of the region of Lower Liptov can be admired.
Basic route: Start at the lower end of the village of **Vyšný Sliač** (550 m). Turn left to the first street leading to the east. The street later changes into field road running along the **Nature Reserve of Sliačske travertíny**. After having seen the remarkable travertine forms on waterlogged meadow return back to the field road, which ascends to the **Čertovica saddle** (625 m). The road descends to the village of Partizánska Ľupča. But the route turns left onto the subsidiary road heading to the north, which ascends to the moderate slope of the comparatively low hill of **Hvozdec** (639 m). The road runs on

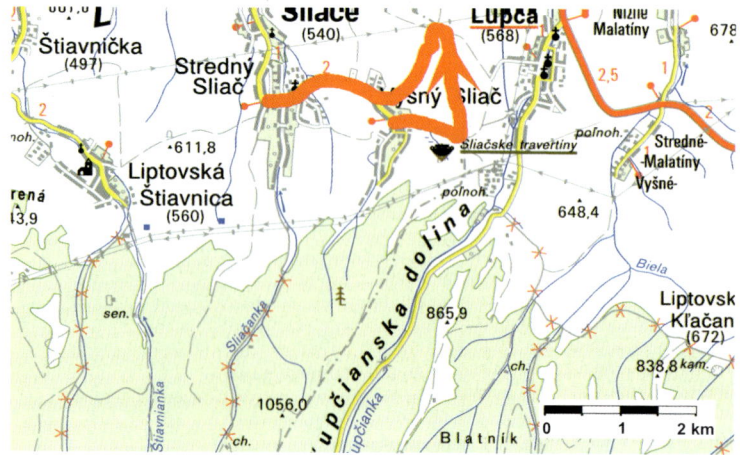

the flat ridge of the hills to the north. The open landscape offers magnificent views of the Liptovská kotlina basin. The cone-shaped Veľký Choč Mt. dominates in the northern horizon. After more than a kilometre you will arrive at the field road. Turn left and the route leading southward from the highest point of this part of hills called **Bežan** (670 m) heads to the road with asphalt surface. Turning left you will return to Vyšné Sliače. Once in the village turn right and the following asphalt road will carry you to the centre of the village, and bus stop at the part called **Stredný Sliač** (540 m).

Options: The short option of the tour contains only the visit to Sliačske travertíny rocks with return to the salient point (total 1 hour). You can vary the basic route by abandoning it below the Bežan.

The travertine rocks of Sliač

42 The Ďurková Mt. from Magurka
Magurka – Ďurková – Zámostská hoľa – Magurka

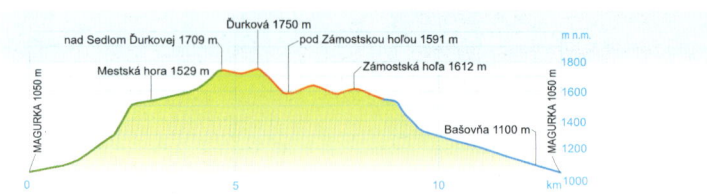

Situation: The Nízke Tatry Mts. – North (western part).
Starting and finishing point: Magurka, parking lot.
Time schedule: Magurka - Mestská hora 1 h - Sedlo Ďurková-crossroads 1 h - Ďurková ¼ h - pod Zámostskou hoľou ½ h - Zámostská hoľa ¼ h - Pri Bašovni 1 ¾ h - Magurka ¼ h. **Total:** 5 hours.
Elevation gain: 700 m.
Map: Nízke Tatry - Chopok 1 : 50 000 (sheet 122), VKÚ, š. p., Harmanec.

Classification: Moderately difficult high-mountain tour with short and steep ascent to the ridge and descent from the ridge.
Basic route: Start at the mountain village of **Magurka** (1,050 m) going up the valley of Ďurková on cart road marked in green (5609). You will be passing by the ski track with a lift on your right. About a kilometre beyond the last houses of the village turn off the road onto the path, which ascends in the steep slope of the mountain ridge of Javorina. The new route of the path avoids the head of the Ďurková valley threatened by snow avalanches in winter. The old path was damaged by disastrous avalanche in 1970. The new path leads to the grassy **Mestská hora Mt.** (1,529 m). Long and mild ascent from the Mestská hora will carry you to the main ridge of the Nízke Tatry Mts. Forest calamities, which destroyed the canopy, opened the view of the region of lower Liptov and the main ridge of the mountain range. Continue as far as the crossroads above the **Sedlo Ďurková** saddle (1,709 m). If you decide to have a rest and refreshment you can visit the restored shelter of Ďurková. descending on green-marked path to the opposite side of the ridge and then return back to the crossroads. Continue from the cross-

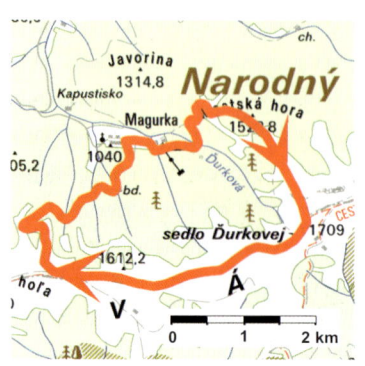

The Magurka Mt.

roads turning left and crossing the Sedlo Ďurková saddle you will easily ascend to the **Ďurková Mt.** (1,750 m), which is not far from there. The way to it is marked by red hiking marks (E8, 0801). Descend from the Ďurková by a short switchback to the lower section of the main ridge and continue slightly descending to the shallow saddle of **Pod Zámostskou hoľou** (1,591 m), where the ridge trail crosses with the path marked in yellow, which connects Magurka in the north with the Jasenianska dolina valley in the south. You, however, will have to continue further to the west and after passing the **Zámostská hoľa Mt.** (1,612 m) walking in slightly undulated section of the ridge you will get to the crossroads **Pod Zámostskou hoľou** (1,560 m). Once there, turn right onto the path marked in blue (2706). The route of descent leads along several old mining shafts and other remains of mining activity. The first stretch descends abruptly down the grassy slope with islands of dwarf pine forest as far as the upper timber line. The path obliquely traverses the slope divided by a series of steep valleys dropping down to the valley of Ďurková. After almost two hours of descent you will arrive at the **Pri Bašovni** crossroads where your route joins the yellow-marked path (8448) coming from the Zámostská hoľa Mt. The descent ends at the settlement of **Magurka**.

43 The Salatín Mt. from Ludrová

Ludrová – Hučiaky – Salatín – Ludrová

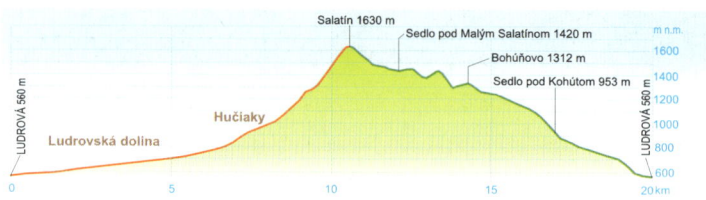

Situation: The Nízke Tatry Mts. – North (western part).
Starting and finishing point: Ludrová, bus stop, parking lot.
Time schedule: Ludrová - Hučiaky 1 ½ h - Magura 1 ¼ h - Salatín 1 ¼ h - Sedlo pod Malým Salatínom ½ h - Bohúňovo ½ h - Sedlo pod Kohútom ½ h - Ludrová ¾ h. **Total:** 6 ¼ hours.
Elevation gain: 1,070 m.
Map: Nízke Tatry - Chopok 1 : 50 000 (sheet 122), VKÚ, š. p., Harmanec.

The valley of Hučiaky

Classification: Moderately difficult tour with short stay in high-mountain environment. Apart from steep ascent to the Salatín Mt. and the following steep descent the remaining stretches are easy. Orientation in prevailingly forest landscape is comparatively simple even in bad weather conditions.
Basic route: Start from the village of **Ludrová** (560 m). Red-marked trail will lead you up the Ludrovská dolina valley. Asphalt road offers an easy and comparatively rapid progress towards the cottage below the crest of the Magura Mt., at the point where the valleys branch. Leaving the cottage behind, turn

left to the valley of dolina **Hučiaky**, which was modelled in the karstic limestone by the torrent of Mraznica. The valley in its lower part acquires the nature of romantic gorge. The valley widens beyond the bend and simultaneously becomes steeper. Immediately below the crest the path crosses mountain meadows called Žliebky. The opportunity to relax before the extremely steep ascent to the top of the Salatín Mt. (1,630 m) comes when you reach the almost levelled top of the crest of **Magura**. Some of the limestone rocks have to be climbed with great effort. The ascent beyond the tallest spruce trees, further into the zone of dwarf pine forest reveals the greatest assets of this isolated cliff. You can get the best views of the region of Liptov from this top. Return from the top of the **Salatín Mt**. following the green marks (5609). The path descends to the northern side of the mountain where there is snow left even in late spring months. The path runs in forest and requires concentration on hiking marks. Descend to the grassy saddle followed by the ascent in fairly confusing terrain and this stretch ends in the shallow saddle of **Sedlo pod Malým Salatínom** (1,420 m).

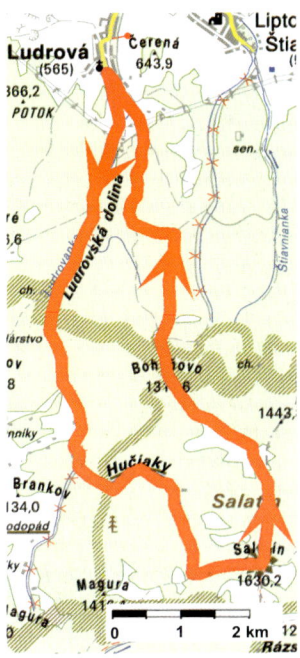

Unmarked path turns right from the saddle and it heads to the top of the Malý Salatín Mt. (1,444 m). The route of your descent continues on the smooth crest of Úplazy (1,428 m) with magnificent views of the top pyramid of the Salatín Mt. The path leaves Úplazy descending through the dwarf pine forest to spruce forest onto the cliff of **Bohúňovo** (1,312 m). Then the path continues over the alpine meadows of the **Kriváň Mt.** (1,233 m) followed by moderately descending forested ridge as far as the **Sedlo pod Kohútom** saddle (953 m). Turn left at the saddle and continue following the green mark. First use the path abruptly descending to the Ludrovská dolina valley, which turns to the right and descends to the edge of the forest. The path is not altogether discernible in the following meadows and pastures, and some of the hiking marks are missing. But it is no problem to find the way to the village as it is lying right in front of you. Descend to the village of **Ludrová** (560 m) passing by the spring of excellent mineral water.

44 The Salatín Mt. from Železné

Železné – Salatín – Liptovská Lúžna

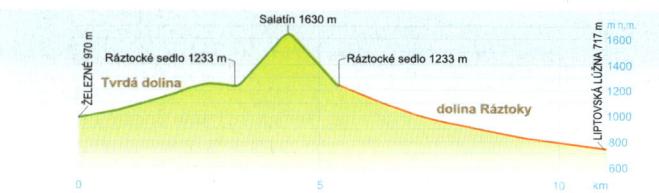

Situation: The Nizke Tatry Mts. – North (western part).
Starting point: Železné, parking lot.
Finishing point: Liptovská Lúžna, bus stop, parking lot.
Time schedule: Železné - Ráztocké sedlo 1 ¼ h - Salatín 1 h - Ráztocké sedlo ¾ h - Liptovská Lúžna 1 ¼ h.
Total: 4 ¼ hours.
Elevation gain: 913 m.
Map: Nízke Tatry - Chopok 1 : 50 000 (sheet 122), VKÚ, š. p., Harmanec.

Classification: Medium difficult tour with short and steep ascent to the ridge and the descent is likewise demanding. The tour starts with steep ascent and ends with steep descent. The crest of the side ridge is rather flat. Some sections of the trek in the forest require concentration from the point of view of orientation. Do not abandon the trail as you can end up in difficult terrain.

Basic route: Start at the mountain village of **Železné** (970 m) walking about a half kilometre on main road in the direction of Partizánska Ľupča. Follow the green marks (5609). Turn left at the bend onto cart road ascending up the Tvrdá dolina valley. The valley branches next to hunter's hut. The route of the ascent heads to the right branch of the valley. When you reach the place where the valley bends ascend to the shallow saddle in the ridge of the Veľký Železný Mt. (1,294 m) and traverse to the wide grassy saddle of **Ráz-**

The Salatín Mt.

tocké sedlo (1,233 m). The most difficult part of the tour starts at this saddle. The ascent up the steep slope is strenuous. Its lower part leads in the forest and the upper part runs alternatively on grass and stony rib. The profile becomes milder only in its final stretch. Passing the grassy terrace you will get to the place where southern and western ridges of the Salatín Mt. join. A short walk in thick dwarf pine forest will carry you to the main top of the **Salatín Mt.** (1,630 m). The beginning of the descent traces the trail of ascent to the **Ráztocké sedlo** saddle. The exposed descent allows visual contact with the tall central ridge of the Nízke Tatry Mts. between the Prašivá and Chopok Mts. The trail descending from the grassy Ráztocké sedlo saddle on the red trail (0854) is not so steep and demanding. It runs in the forest, through pastures to the valley of Ráztoky, which bends after three kilometres to the south where there is also the aim of the trip, the typical village of **Liptovská Lúžna** (717 m) with conserved folk architecture.

Options: You can also continue from the Salatín following the red mark over the Hučiaky to the Ludrovská dolina valley (the contrary direction to that of the trip No. 43) and ends in the village of Ludrová (total 6 hours).

45 The Brankov Mt. and Brankovský vodopád

Biely Potok – Ostré – Brankov – Brankovský vodopád – Podsuchá

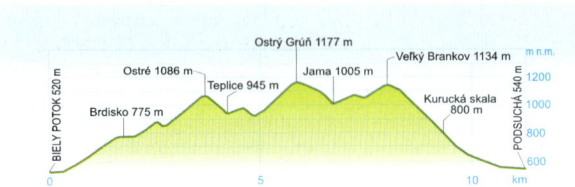

Situation: The Nízke Tatry Mts. – North (western part).
Starting point: Biely Potok, bus stop, parking lot.
Finishing point: Podsuchá, bus stop, parking lot.
Time schedule: Biely Potok - Brdisko ¾ h - Ostré ¾ h - Teplice ¼ h - Brankov 1 h - Jama ½ h - Veľký Brankov ½ h - Brankovský vodopád ½ h - Podsuchá 1 h.
Total: 5 ¼ hours.
Elevation gain: 657 m.
Map: Nízke Tatry - Chopok 1 : 50 000 (sheet 122), VKÚ, š. p., Harmanec.

Classification: Moderately difficult tour with short and steep ascent to the ridge and likewise steep and short descent from it.
Basic route: Start from the bus stop in the settlement of **Biely potok** (520 m), which is now urban district of Ružomberok, cross the bridge eastward onto the street leading parallel to the main road. Follow the green hiking marks (5605). Turn into the northernmost lane, which later joins the path ascending the western slope of the Brankov Mt. Before you reach the forest the views backward encompass the mountain range of the Veľká Fatra. The path ascends to the **Brdisko** saddle (755 m). The path turning left and marked by subsidiary hiking marks heads to the top of the **Borovnisko Mt.** (866 m), which also offers nice views. Return to the original path and continue passing the Brankovský hrebeň ridge in southern direction. Steep ascent to the flatter stretch of the crest of **Kutiny Mt.** (889 m) follows. You will reach the top rock of the **Ostrý Mt.** (1,086 m) walking on the flat forested crest

with a short final ascent. Heavy fighting took place here between the Slovak partisans and German troops in 1944, the reason why the Ostrý Mt. is also referred to as "the Slovak Alcazar". The path descends from the Ostrý to the **Teplice** saddle (945 m). Turning left onto the yellow mark at the crossroads one can have a look at the monument of the Slovak National Uprising in the Ludrovská dolina valley. The route, however, continues southward on top of the narrow crest. The ascent to the most interesting stretch of the ridge trail follows. You will be gradually passing through all tops and shallow saddles within the massive **Brankov Mt.** with more views of the Veľká Fatra Mts. and the Salatín Mt. The northern top of the **Ostrý grúň Mt.** (1,177 m) is the first. Steep descent ends at the grassy saddle called **Jama** (1,005 m) and then the central top also known as Rebro follows. The southern top called Čierny vrch or **Veľký Brankov** (1,134 m) is the last. Descend down the grassy ridge. It turns to the west and the path copies the bend, descending to the gorge-like valley of Veľký Brankov. The path passes bellow the Kurucká skala rock (800 m). The **Brankovský vodopád** waterfall can be seen on one of the rock galleries. You should see it in springtime when it is filled with snow thaw water falling from the height of 55 m. The descent from the top of the Brankov Mt. ends at the bus stop at the village of **Podsuchá** (540 m).

Options: You can shorten the tour if you turn left at the saddle of Teplice and descend following the yellow mark down the Ludrovská dolina valley (total 3 ½ hours).

The Brankovský vodopád waterfall

46 The Nízke Tatry ridge trail (1st part)

Donovaly – Kozí chrbát – Veľká Chochuľa – Ďurková – shelter below Sedlo Ďurková

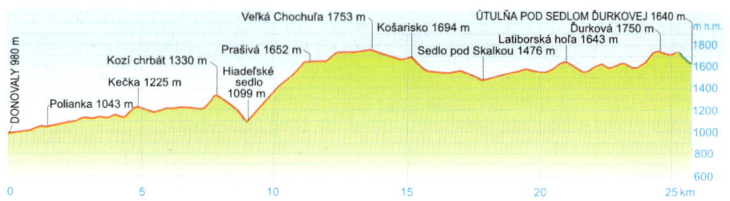

Situation: The Starohorské vrchy Mts., the Nízke Tatry Mts. – western part.
Starting point: Donovaly, bus stop, parking lot.
Finishing point: Shelter below Sedlo Ďurková.
Time schedule: Donovaly - Kečka 1 ¾ h - Kozí chrbát 1 h - Hiadeľské sedlo ½ h - Veľká Chochuľa 2 ¼ h - Sedlo pod Skalkou 1 ¼ h - Latiborská hoľa 1 ¼ h - Zámostská hoľa ¾ h - Ďurková 1 ¼ hod - shelter below Sedlo Ďurková ½ h.
Total: 10 ½ hours.
Elevation gain: 773 m.
Map: Okolie Banskej Bystrice - Donovaly, Nízke Tatry - Chopok 1 : 50 000 (sheet 100, 122), VKÚ, š. p., Harmanec.

Classification: Difficult and very strenuous tour thanks to its large altitude difference and length. It is recommended to start at the dawn. After the demanding ascent from the Hiadeľské sedlo saddle to the crest of the Prašivá Mt., the profile of this ridge trail remains more or less balanced and maintains its altitude above sea level except for one saddle where it drops below 1,500 m. Orientation is on acceptable level. There are no shelter or refreshment available on the route, the last opportunity to refill water is above the Hiadeľské sedlo saddle and after only in the final part of the tour in the shelter below the Sedlo Ďurková saddle. You have to overnight in you own sleeping bag.
Basic route: Red hiking marks (E8, 0801) of the Cesta hrdinov SNP road will show you the way during the whole trip apart from the final stretch descending to the shelter bellow the Sedlo Ďurková. Start at the **Donovaly** (980 m) going southward. The initial part of the tour is on asphalt road, which slightly ascends to the slope on the western edge of the ski tracks below the Baník Mt. The paved road ends in the village of **Polianka** (1,043 m). Somewhat steeper forest road passes into the forested slope of the plain called Barania hlava. While on the plain the path maintains sea level altitude of about 1,030 m. After the moderate descent to the grassy **Moštenické sedlo** saddle (1,050 m) a short steep ascent to the **Kečka Mt.** (1,225 m) follows. Niece views of environs will also accompany you while walking on the tallest crest of the Starohorské vrchy Mts. as far as the Hiadeľské sedlo saddle. The marked path leads

The Prašivá Mt.

over the tallest peak, the **Kozí chrbát Mt.** (1,330 m) of this mountain range. The most difficult stretch is that after the **Hiadeľské sedlo** saddle (1,099) when you enter the territory of the Nízke Tatry mountain range. The ascent to the Prašivá Mt. (1,651 m) is strenuous and long. It leads from the zone of forest to that of dwarf pine and alpine meadows on high mountain ridge. The ascent becomes milder only close below the top of the **Prašivá** (1,652 m) which is 500 m higher than the Hiadeľské sedlo saddle. Steep dropping slopes on both sides of the sharp crest of the Prašivá group will not let you lose your way even if the visibility is low. After climbing the Malá Chochuľa Mt. (1,719 m) you will also ascend the highest point of the tour, **Veľká Chochuľa Mt.** (1,753 m). The grassy ridge slightly descend from the Veľká Chochuľa Mt. over the

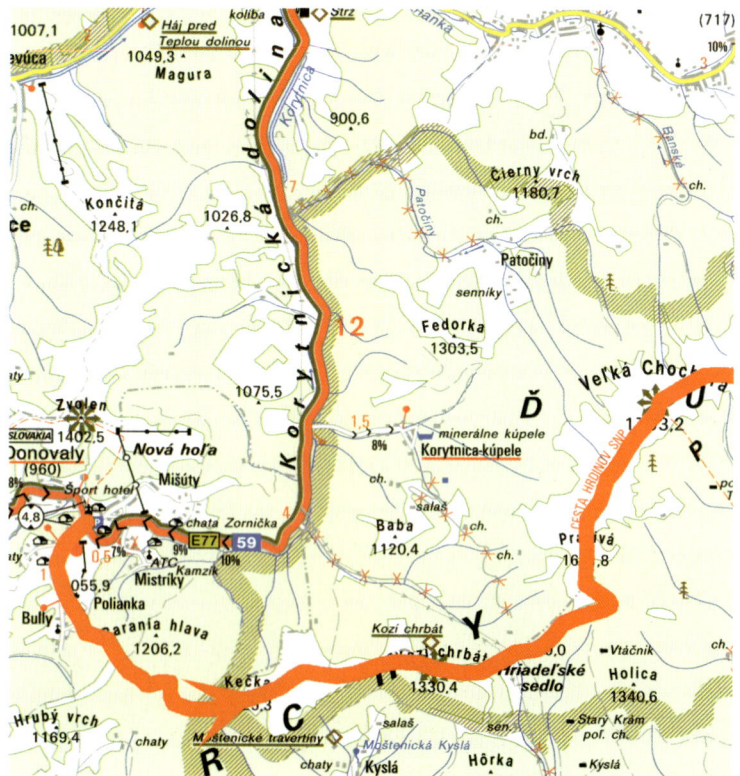

Košarisko and Skalka Mts. to the shallow saddle **Sedlo pod Skalkou** (1,476 m). Yellow-marked path descends from here to Liptovská Lužná. You, however, follow the ridge trail, which ascends now to the Veľká Hoľa Mt. (1,640 m), without reaching its top. The last top is the wide **Latiborská hoľa Mt.** (1,643 m) accessible by steep path and the ascent is more demanding now. Descending pass by the crossroads with the blue-marked trail and continue to the **Zámostská hoľa Mt.** (1,612 m). Descent to shallow saddle with yellow-marked hiking trail and milder stretch on the crest ended by steeper ascent to the **Ďurková Mt.** (1,750 m) follow. Then there is the descent first to the Sedlo Ďurková saddle (1,709 m) and following the green mark another descent to the **shelter below the Sedlo Ďurková** saddle (1,640 m).

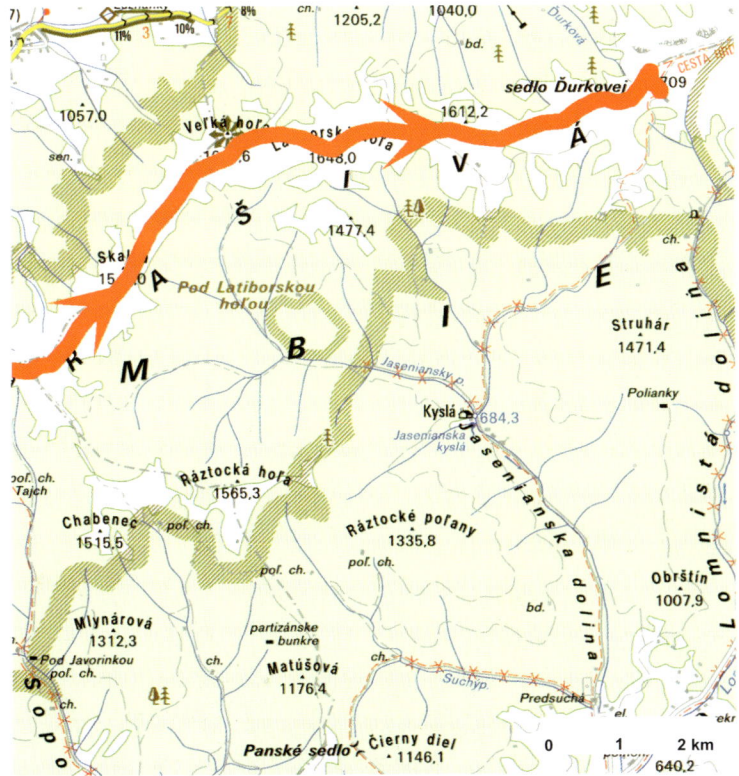

47 The Nízke Tatry ridge trail (2nd part)

Shelter below Sedlo Ďurková – Chabenec – Chopok – Ďumbier – Chata gen. M. R. Štefánika

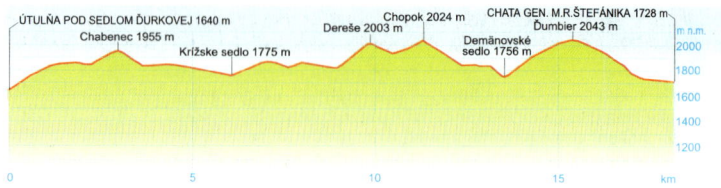

Situation: The Nízke Tatry Mts. - western part.
Starting point: Shelter below Sedlo Ďurková.
Finishing point: Chata gen. M. R. Štefánika.
Time schedule: Shelter below Sedlo Ďurková - Chabenec 1 ¼ h - Kotliská ¾ h - Poľana ¾ h - Dereše 1 ½ h - Chopok ¾ h - Krúpova hoľa 1 ¾ h - Ďumbier ¾ h - Krúpova hoľa-crossroads ½ h - Chata gen. M. R. Štefánika ¾ h.
Total: 8 ¾ hours.
Elevation gain: 403 m.
Map: Nízke Tatry - Chopok 1 : 50 000 (sheet 122), VKÚ, š. p., Harmanec.

Classification: Difficult and very strenuous tour more for its length than altitude difference. It is recommended to start at the dawn. You have to count with all-day stay in high-mountain environment. The grade of the tour is even more demanding in bad weather and poor visibility (which is only too often). The only point of the route providing shelter is the Kamenná chata cottage at the Chopok Mt. Long and strenuous stretches of descent from the main ridge, if you decide for them, are those between the Chabenec and Poľana Mts.

Basic route: The second day on the ridge will be very demanding and long. This is the reason why you should start at dawn. Leaving the **shelter below the**

Sedlo Ďurková saddle (1,640 m) there is a long ascent to the round top of the **Chabenec Mt.** (1,955 m). Follow the red hiking marks (E8, 0801). Continue from the Chabenec Mt. on the sharp crest to the **Kotliská Mt.** (1,937 m) with the side ridge of Skalka, the tallest side ridge of the Nízke Tatry Mts. The surrounding landscape becomes wilder and steep slopes dropping into what were originally glacier valleys limit the ridge. Cliffs towering above the dark glacier kettles are situated mostly on the northern side. The tour descends abruptly from the Kotliská Mt. to the **Krížske sedlo** saddle (1,775 m) and ascends again of the **Poľana Mt.** (1,890 m). Leaving the Poľana Mt. behind you will get to the highest situated stretch of the main ridge above the head of the Demänovská dolina valley. You can comparatively quickly descend from the Sedlo Poľana saddle (1,837 m) to the Vrbické pleso lake following the yellow hiking marks. But the ridge trail continues by moderate ascent to the first two-thousand metre tall peaks of our trip: the **Dereše Mt.** (2,003 m) and **Chopok Mt.** (2,024 m). The path avoids the top of the Dereše Mt., but if you ascend it you will be rewarded by far-reaching views of the surrounding landscape. Ascending the top of the Chopok Mt. you will get the rare opportunity of refreshment at the Kamenná chata cottage. The tall eastern top of the Chopok Mt. above the cottage provides the best views. The chair lifts connecting both sides of the mountain with the valley are out of use. Continue on your ridge trail, this stretch is comparatively a much visited one, the path is wide and well-discernible. You can meet swarms of tourists here in any season. Now you are slightly descending to the **Demänovské sedlo** saddle (1,756 m). You will reach the **Krúpova hoľa Mt.** (1,927 m) by a short ascent from the distinct depression between the couple of the best known peaks of the Nízke Tatry Mts., the Chopok and Ďumbier (2,043 m). You should not miss the opportunity to visit also this tallest peak of the Nízke Tatry. More so, if the weather is good as its top provides a complete panoramic view. After returning back to the crossroads below **Krúpova hoľa Mt.** the hiking path traversing the southern slope of the **Ďumbier Mt.** covered by debris will carry you to the aim of the second day´s trip, the **Chata gen. M. R. Štefánika** cottage (1,728 m). This high-mountain

Dereše

cottage at the saddle on the southern foothill of the Ďumbier Mt. accessible only on foot, is open the whole year round and offers both refreshment and accommodation.

Options: Options are, also in this case, the ways to leave the trek in case of emergency. The first option to do so is to descend from above the Sedlo Ďurková saddle on green-marked path to Magurka (1 ¼ hours). The descent on green-marked path from the shelter below the Sedlo Ďurková saddle going southward to Jasenie is substantially longer (3 ¼ hours). Leaving the ridge at Kotliská turning right on yellow mark is not recommended either. Large portion of it runs on deserted risky terrain and it takes four hours to get to Krpáčovo. The next yellow turning to the left at the Poľana Mt. is not suitable for rapid retreat from the main ridge. It is rather recommended to turn off sooner, at the Krížske sedlo saddle onto the right blue-marked trail, which traverses the southern slope as far as Kosodrevina (1 ¾ hours) or in the Sedlo Poľana saddle take the yellow turning to the left which descends down the valley to Jasná (2 hours).

Kotliská

48 The Nízke Tatry ridge trail (3rd part)
Chata gen. M. R. Štefánika – Čertovica – Bacúšske sedlo – shelter of Ramža

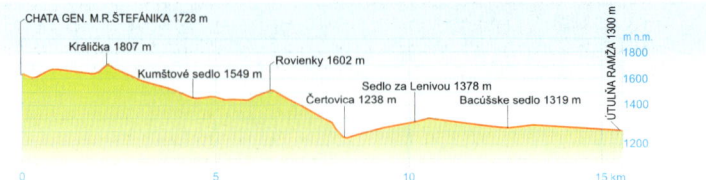

Situation: The Nízke Tatry Mts. - eastern part.
Starting point: Chata gen. M. R. Štefánika.
Finishing point: Shelter of Ramža.
Time schedule: Chata gen. M. R. Štefánika - Králička ¾ h - Kumštové sedlo ¾ h - Rovienky ½ h - Čertovica ¾ h - Sedlo za Lenivou ¾ h - Bacúšske sedlo ¾ h - shelter of Ramža ¾ h.
Total: 5 hours. **Elevation gain:** 569 m.
Map: Nízke Tatry - Chopok, Nízke Tatry - Kráľova hoľa 1 : 50 000 (sheet 122, 123), VKÚ, š. p., Harmanec.

Classification: Medium difficult high-mountain tour with comparatively low altitude difference. It should be a kind of rest after the first two strenuous days of trekking. The Čertovica saddle offers opportunity of refreshment and provision. This part of the tour ends at the shelter called Ramža in the main ridge of the Kráľovohoľské Tatry Mts. above the head of the Bacúšska dolina valley. It is accessible only on foot, you can overnight only in your own sleeping bag. There is also a spring with drinking water.

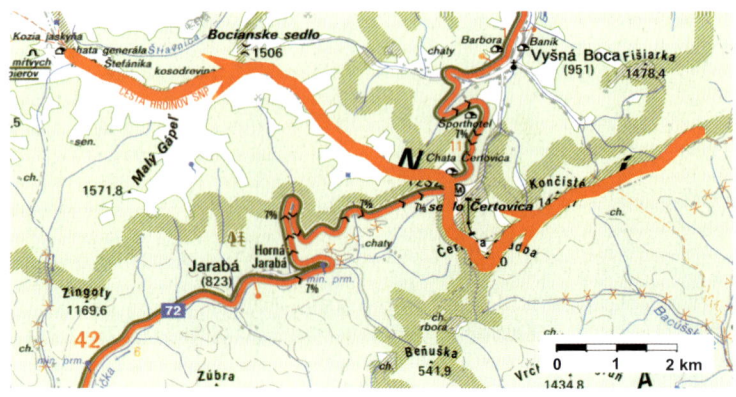

Basic route: The third day of passage over the main ridge of the mountain range starts at the **Chata gen. M. R. Štefánika** cottage (1,728 m). Red hiking marks (E8, 0801) will guide you the whole day. The initial stretch is comparatively flat. Only the short ascent to the slope of the **Králičky Mt.** (1,807 m), which is also the highest point of the tour, is an exception. The path avoids the top from the left side and continues by moderate descent to the **Panská hoľa Mt**. (1,635 m). A bit steeper descent will carry you to the **Kumštové sedlo** saddle (1,549 m) where the ridge trail crosses with the green-marked trail. The grassy mountains give way to thick dwarf pine canopy. Leaving the **Rovienky Mt.** (1,602 m) behind you will find yourself again on grassy surface. The crest of the **Lajštroch Mt.** you can enjoy the beautiful view of the Kráľovohoľské Tatry Mts. as you are drawing closer to them. The route becomes steeper and you are now entering the forest. There is an opportunity of short rest and refreshment at the saddle of **Čertovica** (1,238 m). If you can, provide yourself as there is no other opportunity to do so before the end of the ridge tour. As you are leaving the busy saddle of Čertovica behind, you enter ever deeper into the forest. Slightly ascending comfortable road avoids the Čertova svadba Mt. (1,463 m). The red-marked trail turns to the north-east at the crossroads **Sedlo za Lenivou** (1,378 m). It avoids the higher situated ridge culminating by the Končistá Mt. (1,474 m). You will return temporarily to the ridge at the **Bacúšske sedlo** saddle (1,319 m) where our trail crosses with the blue-marked hiking trail. The route continues from the Bacúšske sedlo saddle eastward in thick woods, in places interrupted by clearings and alpine meadows. At the edge of the **shelter of Ramža** (1,300 m) stands an open log hut.

The Lajštroch Mt.

49 The Nízke Tatry ridge trail (4th part)

Shelter of Ramža – Homôľka – Veľká Vápenica – shelter below Andrejcová

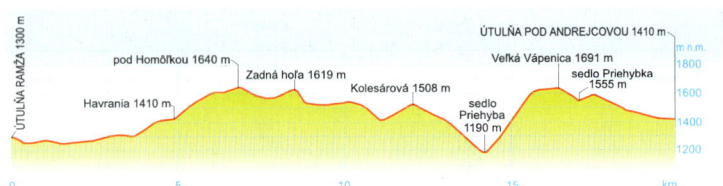

Situation: The Nízke Tatry Mts. - eastern part.
Starting point: Shelter of Ramža.
Finishing point: Shelter below Andrejcová.
Time schedule: Shelter of Ramža - Havrania 1 ¼ h - Zadná hoľa 1 h - Kolesárová 1 ¼ h - Priehyba 1 h - Veľká Vápenica 1 ¾ h - Priehybka ¼ h - shelter below Andrejcová 1 h.
Total: 7 ½ hours.
Elevation gain: 501 m.
Map: Nízke Tatry - Kráľova hoľa 1 : 50 000 (sheet 123), VKÚ, š. p., Harmanec.

Classification: Moderately difficult high-mountain tour with comparatively low altitude difference. Short and comfortable descents leading to the southern side of the mountain range are the suitable ways of retreat.
Basic route: Starting at the **shelter of Ramža** (1,300 m) continue in the passage of the ridge of the Nízke Tatry Mts. on the route marked in red hiking marks (E8, 0801). Its initial part runs on the southern side of the main ridge. The ridge trail traverses the uppermost part of the ridge slope in the head of the branched Bacúšska dolina valley. It passes through the alpine meadow of **Havrania,** beyond which the well-discernible path ascends in the slope of the **Homôľka** Mt. (1,660 m). Traverse the proper top on its southern hillside. Short detour should remind you that the Nízke Tatry Mts. are rich in mountain tops with wonderful views. Ascend from the grassy saddle of **Homôľka** (1,570 m) through the dwarf pine belt as far as the **Zadná hoľa Mt.** (1,619 m) on the green/red-marked trail. The yellow mark turns left

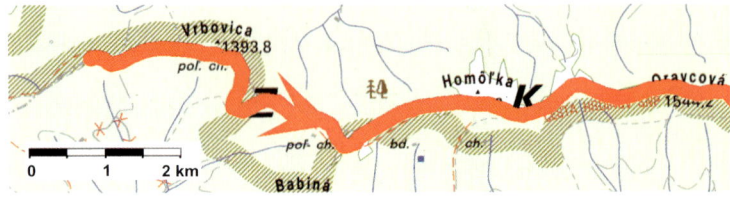

at the Zadná hoľa Mt. and it leads to the massive karstic mountain of Veľký bok (1,727 m). Further east the ridge trail continues through undulated meadows and forest across the Oravcová Mt. (1,544 m) to the **Kolesárová Mt**. (1,508 m). The alpine meadows east of it opens wonderful views of the environs. Thanks to them you can see the final stretch of the tour dominated by the Veľká Vápenica Mt. But before you start the strenuous ascent in its steep western slope you have to descend down the forested crest to the **Priehyba** saddle (1,190 m). At the saddle you will cross the cart road

The Andrejcová Mt.

between the villages of Heľpa and Čierny Váh. The demanding climb up the **Veľká Vápenica Mt**. (1,691 m) is finally compensated by the unique panoramic view. The descent to the eastern side is substantially more rapid and comfortable. Go down the old road to the shallow high situated saddle of **Priehybka** (1,555 m). The last, rather unpleasant but short section of the tour, is the ascent in rocky terrain to not very high Heľpiansky vrch Mt. (1,586 m). Having it overcome there is only the final half-an-hour comfortable walk to the **shelter below Andrejcová** (1,410 m). This tourist shelter on the alpine meadow near the eponymous mountain at the central part of the main ridge of the Kráľovohoľské Tatry Mts. is the traditional one where the hikers overnight. It provides simple accommodation for 15 tourists who bring their own sleeping bags. There is a spring nearby.

Options: There are several options of precipitated retreat from the ridge. The saddle of Homôlka offers one of them as you can descend to Polomka (2 ¾ hours). Blue-marked path descends from the Oravcová crossroads to the village of Závadka nad Hronom (2 ½ hours).

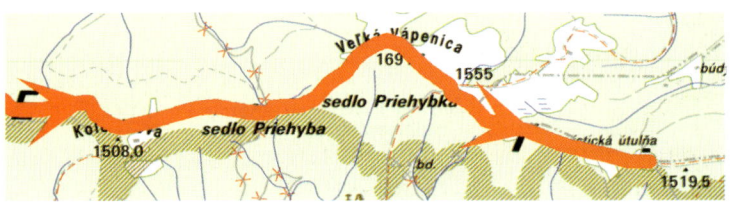

50 The Nízke Tatry ridge trail (5th part)
Shelter below Andrejcová – Orlová – Kráľova hoľa – Telgárt

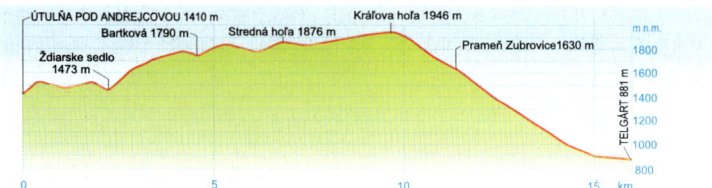

Situation: The Nízke Tatry Mts. - eastern part.
Starting point: Shelter below Andrejcová.
Finishing point: Telgárt, bus stop, railway station, parking lot.
Time schedule: Shelter below Andrejcová - Ždiarske sedlo ½ h - Orlová 1 ½ h - Kráľova hoľa 1 ¼ h - Prameň Zubrovice ½ h - Telgárt 1 ½ h. **Total:** 5 ¼ hours.
Elevation gain: 1,065 m.
Map: Nízke Tatry - Kráľova hoľa 1: 50 000 (sheet 123), VKÚ, š. p., Harmanec.

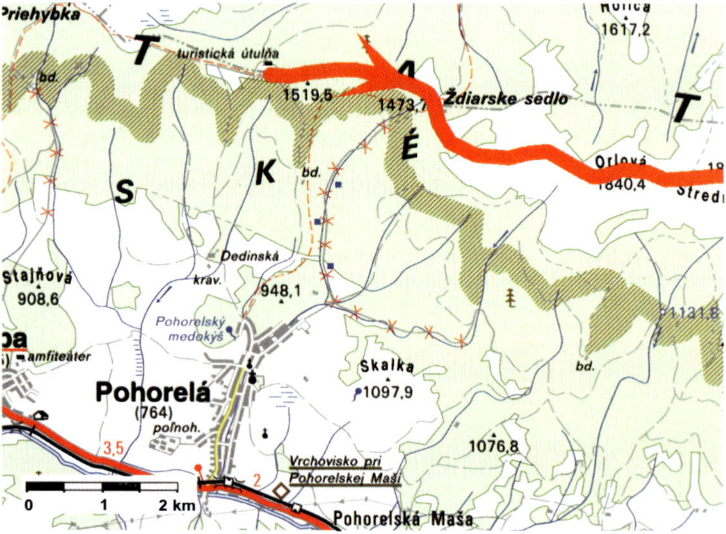

Classification: Moderately difficult high-mountain tour, low altitude difference and long and exposed descent from the Kráľova hoľa Mt. to Telgárt.
Basic route: Start from the **shelter below Andrejcová** (1,410 m) eastward following the red hiking marks (E8, 0801). After passing the eponymous alpine meadow situated on the top descend to the shallow **Ždiarske sedlo** saddle (1,473 m). If you choose the blue mark at the crossroads you should arrive at Pohorelá (right turning) or to Liptovská Teplička (left turning). Your route though, is marked in red and it will take you to the steep slope of the highest part of the Kráľovohoľské Tatry Mts. You will be moving in high-mountain environment until reaching the eastern slope of the Kráľova hoľa Mt. Gradually climb the trio of elevations within the main ridge, the height of which grows going from the west to the east: the **Bartková Mt.** (1,790 m), **Orlová Mt.** (1,840 m), and **Stredná hoľa** (1,876 m). The path runs alternatively in grass and on stones. Pay attention to the marking, it is sometimes painted on stones. Unwanted movement on steep hillside of the northern kettles overgrown with impenetrable dwarf pine canopy is particularly unpleasant. The ridge becomes wider and rounder when you leave the Stredná hoľa Mt. behind. The TV tower on top of the legendary **Kráľova hoľa Mt.** (1,946 m) shows you the way. You will get an unforgettable view of the High Tatras and the Západné Tatry Mts. if you climb the rocks. There are five descending routes down from the top of the Kráľova hoľa Mt. Stick to the red

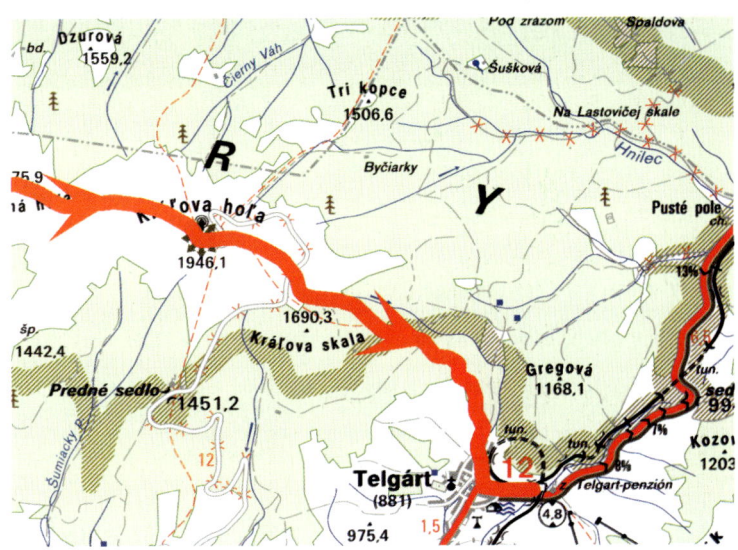

The Kráľova hoľa Mt.

mark. The upper part of your route of descent crosses twice the asphalt road leading to Šumiac, the village lying on the southern foothill of the Kráľova hoľa Mt. The **Prameň Zubrovica** spring (1,630 m) offering fresh drinking water is next to the second crossing. Continue along the Zubrovica brook, On the right side of the trail is the cliff called Kráľova skala rock. After a while you enter the spruce forest. The descent is comparatively steep and unpleasant apart from several short traverses. The final stretch turns to left and ends in the village of **Telgárt** (881 m). Turning left on the main road you will arrive at the railway station, which is the final point of the 5th part of the ridge tour in the Nízke Tatry Mts.

Options: Options are in fact the ways how to leave the main ridge. You can do so directly next to the Andrejcová shelter if you descend on the yellow path to Pohorelá (2 ½ hours). The blue-marked path diverges at the Ždiarske sedlo saddle and it leads to Liptovská Teplička (3 hours). But the right branch of the blue path ending in Pohorelá (2 ½ hours) is better.

Natural landmarks and points of interests

The Nízke Tatry Mts. - South

The ideal starting point in the south-western part of the Nízke Tatry Mts. is the mountain village of **DONOVALY** (960 m, population 150). Donovaly is the favourite of tourists both in winter and summer. Several marked hiking routes start here and the best known of them is the **Cesta hrdinov SNP** (The Road of Heroes of the Slovak National Uprising) leading along the crests of the Nízke Tatry Mts. It is a delight of passionate hiker as it compensates the toil with unusual and supreme experience. It should be divided into several stretches and into several days passing the nights in mountain hotels and shelters on the ridge or immediately below it (routes No. 46, 47, 48, 49 and 50). The first part can finish, for instance at the Hiadeľské sedlo saddle where there is an option to descend to the highest situated spa in Slovakia: the **Korytnica-kúpele** spa (825 m, route No. 2). The instructive path running across the Starohorské vrchy Mts. to the mining village of **ŠPANIA DOLINA** (710 m, population 150, route No. 1) with surviving folk architecture is also interesting.

The southern slopes of the Nízke Tatry Mts. are interspersed by a number of valleys oriented in the direction of south-north. Perhaps the most interesting valleys lying in the west are the Hiadeľská and Uhliarska dolina, which form a circle suitable for a day-long trip. The starting point of the route (No. 3) is the village of **HIADEĽ** (500 m, population 600). The valley bearing the name of this village is about 10 km long and it separates the Nízke Tatry Mts. from the Starohorské vrchy Mts. Its most interesting landmark is the mineral spring of **Hiadeľská kyslá** located about 2.5 km from the northern head of the mentioned valley. Crossing the Hiadeľské sedlo saddle and the **nature reserve of Kozí chrbát** you can go down to the Zubová saddle and the **natural phenomenon Moštenické travertíny** travertine rocks and mineral spring **Moštenická kyslá**. The descent through the Uhliarska dolina valley ends in a small sub-mountainous village of **MOŠTENICA** (452 m, population 200).

RÁZTOKA (480 m, population 350), lies further to the east and it also can be the starting or final point of different hiking tours. One of the easiest is the walk to **Ráztocké lazy** (route No. 5), while the ascents to the **Ráztocká hoľa Mt.** (1,565 m) or **Veľká Chochuľa Mt.** (1,753 m, route No. 4) are more toilsome. The tops of them provide extensive panoramic views. The red-marked footpath also called the Partisans' Road leads further east from Ráztoky to **JASENIE** (507 m, population 1,150), an ideal starting point to the trips to **Ďurková Mt.** (1,750 m). The path ascends through the **Lomnistá** (route No. 6) or **Jasenianska dolina** valleys. If you continue on the Partisans' Road on the southern foothills of the Nízke Tatry Mts., from Jasenie, you will soon arrive at the recreation settlement of Krpáčovo, the centre of tourism on the foothills of the Ďumbierske Tatry Mts. Numerous hotels, cottages and the water reservoir made **Krpáčovo** the favourite place of summer and winter tourists, especially families with children. They will certainly appreciate the hiking footpaths to Tále (route No. 9) or around the **Prameň of Samo Chalupka** spring (route No. 8) to **HORNÁ LEHOTA** (640 m, population 600) and **DOLNÁ LEHOTA** (480 m, population 750). More demanding and fitter hikers will prefer one of the longest valleys on the southern foothills of the Nízke Tatry Mts., the 20 km long **Vajskovská dolina** valley with impressive scenery, waterfalls and rock faces (route No. 7).

One of the most important recreation and tourist settlements **Tále** (route No. 9) is almost connected with Krpáčovo. Favourable position below the massive Chopok Mt. with ski facilities, a swimming pool, accommodation and catering facilities became very attractive for visitors the same in summer as in winter. Tále is now one of the most frequently visited tourist centre in the Nízke Tatry Mts. and offers numerous hiking options. Hikers love the **Bystrá dolina** valley, which stretches as far as the below the main ridge of the range. State road passes through the valley and connects Tále with **Trangoška** and **Srdiečko**, other recreation villages. Both of them are good starting points for the tours to the tallest summits of the Nízke Tatry Mts.: **Ďumbier** (2,043 m, routes No 11 and 13), **Chopok** (2,024 m, route No. 12), and **Baba** (1,617 m route No. 10). Lovers of hiking will find there several marked footpaths and can choose the one that suits them best. Especially the stretch between the Ďumbier and Chopok Mts. is very attractive and frequented in summer for its unique views of the surrounding landscape. The northern part of the Ďumbier Mt. is the **national nature reserve**, one of the largest in Slovakia (2,044 hectares). The high-mountain karst (let us mention the best known cave of the area, the Jaskyňa mŕtvych netopierov cave with countless cave corridors situated in several horizons, accessible to public). Cliffs and troughs, alpine meadows, mountain dwarf pine canopy and deep forests with abundant vegetation and fauna comprising hundreds of precious and protected species are the elements of nature that provide unforgettable experience to visitors. The accommodation and refreshment facilities in this part of the Nízke Tatry Mts., above all those near the Kamenná chata cottage below the Chopok Mt., the mountain cottage of **Chata gen. Milana Rastislava Štefánika** below the Ďumbier Mt., and the mountain hotels **Kosodrevina**, **Srdiečko** and **Trangoška** are also worth mentioning.

The **Čertovica** saddle and the mountain cottage of Chata gen. M. R. Štefánika, about 7 km away from it, are the favourite and much frequented stops of hikers. There are many options to trips from the saddle of Čertovica. One of the most used routes is that starting at Čertovica and running on

The Vajskovský vodopád waterfall

The Stredná hoľa Mt. from the Kráľova hoľa Mt.

top of the mountain ridge westward with diversion to the **Bocianske sedlo** saddle (1,506 m) and to the **Starobocianska dolina** valley (route No. 14). The trip heading from Čertovica to the east leads to the **Sedlo za Lenivou** saddle (1,434 m) where there is an option to turn onto the green hiking mark (route No. 15 leading to the south to the village of **BRAVÄCOVO** (615 m, population 750). If you decide to continue eastward on the ridge you will soon reach the **Bacúšske sedlo** saddle (1,319 m) where you can turn onto the blue-marked path (route No. 16) southward to the village of **BACÚCH** (629 m, population 1,100) or northward to **VYŠNÁ BOCA** (951 m, population 100).

There are also numerous alternatives of hiking trips in the mountain and high-mountain environment in the eastern part of the Nízke Tatry Mts. on their southern foothills. The forest road leading to the ridge of the Nízke Tatry Mts. starts at the village of **POLOMKA** (628 m, population 3,200). It runs first up the **Ždiarska dolina** valley (route No. 17) ending at the ridge of the mountain range then it continues to the top of the Zadná hoľa Mt. (1,619 m) where there is the option to descend to the village of **ZÁVADKA NAD HRONOM** (627 m, population 2,550). Then there are trips starting in two villages of the valley of the Hron river: **HEĽPA** (695 m, population 3,000) and

POHORELÁ (764 m, population 2,900). The aim of the first trip (route No. 18) is the top of the **Veľká Vápenica Mt.** (1,691 m) with wonderful views, and the highest point of the second trip (route No. 19) is the top of the **Andrejcová Mt.** (1,519 m) with a log shelter for late-comers in emergency.

The dominant of the easternmost part of the Nízke Tatry Mts. is the **Kráľova hoľa Mt.** (1,946 m), which also gave name to the eastern part of the range: the Kráľovohorské Tatry Mts. Its top is accessible by several hiking footpaths. If you want to ascend to the top from its southern side, you must start in **TELGÁRT** (881 m, population 1,600, route No. 20) or **ŠUMIAC** (880 m, population 1,450). Both routes are moderately demanding.

The Nízke Tatry Mts. - North

A longer, more demanding, though perhaps more favourite way to the top of the Kráľova hoľa Mt. is the path starting in **LIPTOVSKÁ TEPLIČKA** (919 m, population 2,200, route No. 21). The green hiking route to the Kráľova hoľa Mt. heads from the village to the south-east. In the Liptovská kotlina basin and later in the valley of the Čierny Váh river it is a comfortable walk. However, the second part of the tour, the ascent from Záturňa (1,302 m) one has to overcome a considerable elevation difference. But the trip and especially the view from the **Kráľova hoľa Mt.** (1,946 m) are worth the toil. The Kráľova hoľa Mt. is a massive mountain and the tallest one of the eastern part of the Nízke Tatry Mts.

The environs of this village also offer little demanding trips and walks. Families should choose the ascent to the **Doštianka Mt.** (1,235 m, route No. 22), the stripped crest with ski tracks. The walk in the valley of the Čierny Váh river or the passage from **LUČIVNÁ** (767 m, population 900, route No. 23) to **VIKARTOVCE** (756 m, population 1,650) lying nearby across the **Kozie chrbty Mts.** are also easy.

Only a few kilometres eastward near the confluence of Biely Váh and Čierny Váh rivers is the village of **KRÁĽOVA LEHOTA** (741 m, population 700). Kráľova Lehota provides an entry to the 35 kilometre long **valley of Čierny Váh**, the longest in the mountain range of the Nízke Tatry mountains. The river Čierny Váh springs below the Kráľova hoľa mountain, at an altitude of 1,680 metres above sea level. In the valley there are two foresters' communities, **Svarín** and **Čierny Váh** (routes No. 24 and 26), known above all because of the **water power station** built on the river, the highest situated one in Slovakia.

Kráľova Lehota lies beyond the busy road communication from Liptov over the Čertovica saddle in the Low Tatra Mts. to Horehronie region. The first village on the road is **MALUŽINÁ** (733 m, population 300). For the lovers of hiking in the quiet and picturesque environment of the Low Tatra Mts., Malužiná has a blue-marked hiking trail up the Malužinská dolina valley.

The blue mark leaves the Malužinská dolina valley later and enters the Hodruša valley. One can continue through the Malužinská dolina valley up to the iron-sulphate spring Malužinská kyselica or Malužinská Acid Water, but the route through Dolina Hodruša valley ending in the Pod Veľkým bokom saddle is more interesting. The remains of the mining road remind of the mining past of the area. Yellow-marked path heads to the south and runs from the saddle to the top of the **Široká Mt.** (1,535 m) and through forest clearings with plenty of blackberries and cowberries further to the top of the Zadná hoľa Mt. (1,620 m) in the main ridge of the Nízke Tatry Mts. From the sedlo pod Veľkým bokom saddle one can go also northward to the cone-shaped top of the **Veľký bok Mt.** (1,727 m). The yellow-marked trail takes you to the ridge of the Nemecká (1,535 m) and continues descending to one of the most picturesque valleys of this part of the Nízke Tatry Mts., the **Svarínska dolina** valley (route No. 25).

The yellow marked path goes also to the west from Malužiná to the Svidovské sedlo saddle (1,135 m) with options to descend to the Jánska dolina valley or to ascend to the top of Ohnište Mt. (1,538 m). The route runs in the national **nature reserve Ohnište** (route No. 27). It protects preserved limestone-dolomite rock formations (the best known is a cliff called **Okno**, ten metres high rock opening and precious plant and animal communities.

There are another two villages in the Bocianska dolina valley: **NIŽNÁ BOCA** (851 m, population 200) and **VYŠNÁ BOCA** (951 m, population 100). Both villages are now known and lot frequented recreation centres with plenty of private cottages and huts. They are ideal starting points for the summer and winter tourism. In winter it is a lively ski resort with several well prepared skiing tracks. The most important ski centre is the **sedlo Čertovica** saddle.

The Čertovica saddle is a good starting point of summer hiking. One of the interesting tours runs from the saddle eastward on the main ridge of the Low Tatras. It is more or less comfortable walk mostly through the forest up to the **Bacúšske sedlo** saddle (1,319 m) with option to descend to Vyšná Boca by the blue-marked trail (route No. 16). Going the opposite direction (route No. 14) one will get to the crest and over the top of the **Lajštroch Mt.** (1,601 m) or as far as at the **Kumštové sedlo** saddle (1,548 m). You can continue turning off onto a green-marked trail leading to the wide **Bocianske sedlo** saddle (1,506 m). You can return to Vyšná Boca from the saddle by the yellow marked trail with nice views of the surrounding landscape dotted with remains of the past mining activity. Or you can ascend from the Bocianske sedlo saddle heading to the north-east by the green-marked path to **Rovná hoľa Mt.** (1,723 m) and return to Nižná Boca descending on the yellow-marked trail running mostly an open terrain with wonderful views (route No. 27).

The final aim for most visitors though is **LIPTOVSKÝ JÁN** (654 m, population 800). Liptovský Ján is the point of departure for the **Jánska dolina** valley, one of the longest valleys in the Low Tatras. It is crossed by a blue-

Nižná Boca

marked footpath leading to the **Chata gen. M. R. Štefánika** cottage lying under the highest point of the Low Tatras, Ďumbier (2,043 m). Out of the valley several hiking tracks (route No. 28, 29, 30) depart offering on their way an opportunity to admire variegated flora, karst phenomena, sinkholes, water springs, caves and abysses in the area.

Since 1964 all existing tourist points of interest in the valley are concentrated in the self-governing village of **DEMÄNOVSKÁ DOLINA** (820 m, population 200). It consists of five small recreation areas: **Tri studničky** in its lower part, **Jaskyne**, **Repiská**, and **Lúčky** in the central part and **Jasná** in the upper part of the valley. Its geomorphologic diversity, rich flora and fauna and friendly climate have also contributed to its popularity among tourists. Over an area of 837 ha extends the **national nature reserve**, the lower part of which is formed by a canyon-like valley of limestone and dolomites. The upper part of the valley has a granite base with a glacier surface (the Vrbické pleso lake, the **national nature reserve** is on one of the moraines) and with a compound of smaller valleys. It is drained by the

Železné

streams Zadná voda and Demänovka, creating with their sinkholes a unique underground system: the **Demänovské jaskyne** caves. The most beautiful and most popular cave, not only in this region, but all over Slovakia is the **Demänovská jaskyňa slobody**. Also the nearby **Demänovská ľadová jaskyňa**, one of first such caves known around the world, is most attractive.

The Demänovská dolina valley offers lovers of hiking ten marked routes (routes No. 31-40) and a thick network of footpaths suitable also for more leisurely walkers. In the lower part of the valley the paths lead across forests and deep canyons interspersed with steep cliffs, contrasted by the upper part, which is dominated by dwarf pine forests and alpine meadows. The majority of the routes are connected into circuits. Tourists in good physical condition almost always use the occasion to ascend to some of the Low Tatra peaks, like **Chopok** (2,024 m) or **Ďumbier** (2,043 m) providing them a superb view of almost half of Slovakia.

Historically more important is the nearby community of **PARTIZÁNSKA ĽUPČA** (568 m, population 1,300), the oldest and once the most famous town of the Liptov region. Partizánska Lupča is also the starting point for tourist trips to the almost 20 km long **Lupčianska dolina** valley (route No. 31) remarkable for its continuous natural forests and abundance of game. There are several gamekeeper's lodges and hunting cottages in the area. The valley has numerous lateral branch routes, of which the most favourite is the valley of the Ďurková brook (blue-marked path) leading from a place called Tajcha, with traces of a valley water reservoir, once used for floating the timber to the small mountain community of **Magurka** (1,036 m, route No. 42). This old community originated in the 14th century around the gold, silver and later antimony and iron ore mines.

Three marked paths lead from Magurka to the main ridge of the Low Tatras. Tourists who lodge at Magurská cottage frequently visit the nearby community of **Železné** (970 m) accessible by a green-marked footpath. There used to be a **climatic spa** in the community in the 19th century used as a summer residence by writers, poets and artists. Among its regular guests was the famous Slovak poet P. O. Hviezdoslav who translated Shakespeare's texts here. Today, besides the mineral water spring, there is also a children's sanatorium.

Returning to Ružomberok, there are several communities in the Liptovská kotlina basin, particularly in the part within the Nízke Tatry Mts. The easternmost of them is **SLIAČE** (550 m, population 3,800, route No. 41) consisting of three localities: Nižný, Stredný and Vyšný Sliač.

South-west of the community of Sliače where the Ludrovská dolina valley ends in the Liptovská kotlina basin, is the community of **LUDROVÁ** (565 m, population 950). However, lovers of nature usually merely pass the community on their way to the Ludrovská dolina valley and go on tracking to the **Salatín mountain** (1,630 m, route No. 43). The red-marked route, comparatively comfortable at the beginning but quite demanding towards the end offers some interesting views of karst phenomena (small narrows, caves, sinkholes, sinking streams) and rare flora species. The Salatín Mt. was declared the national nature reserve in 1980 for its unique botanical and zoological values. Also the rock and karst phenomena in the gorge of Skalné-Hučiaky are attractive. You can go down from the Salatín Mt. over the Ráztocké sedlo saddle (1,231 m) following the red mark as far as to the typical village of **LIPTOVSKÁ LÚŽNA** (717 m, population 3,050, route No. 44).

The starting point for the Nízke Tatry Mts. is the local municipal part of Biely Potok with a tourist footpath marked in green leading to the **Borovnisko mountain** (866 m) with enchanting scenery and views of the Lower Liptov, which continues to the peaks of Ostrý (1,066 m) and **Veľký Brankov** (1,134 m, route No. 45). At the foothills of the latter is the protected **Brankovský vodopád** waterfall, which falls from the height of 55 m.

Register (The entries are followed by numbers of routes)

Andrejcová 19

Baba 10
Bacúch 16
Bacúšske sedlo 16, 48
Bašovňa 42
Beňuška 15
Bežan 41
Biely Potok 45
Bocianske sedlo 14, 25
Bodová 30
Bohúňovo 43
Bôr 35
Brankov 45
Brankovský vodopád 45
Braväcovo 15
Brdisko 45
Brhliská 37
Brusno 4
Bukovinka 15, 17
Bully 1
Bystrina 31

Čertovica 14, 15, 41, 48
Čierny Váh 21
Črchľa 25
Črmné 7, 8

Demänovská dolina 31, 36, 37
Demänovská hora 31
Demänovská jaskyňa mieru 31, 33
Demänovská jaskyňa slobody 33, 34, 35
Demänovská ľadová jaskyňa 31, 32
Demänovské sedlo 11, 38
Dereše 7, 12, 38, 39, 47
Dolná Lehota 8
Donovaly 1, 2, 46
Doštianka 22
Dve vody 7
Ďumbier 11, 13, 29, 47

Hadlanka 3
Halašova jama 11, 13
Havrania 49
Heľpa 18
Hiadeľ 3
Hiadeľská dolina 3
Hiadeľská kyslá 3
Hiadeľské sedlo 2, 3, 46
Hlboká 15
Hodruša 24
Homôlka 17
Horná Lehota 8
Horný Šturec 1
Hrádocký most 26
Hučiaky 43

Chabenec 47
Chata Čertovica 14
Chata gen. M. R. Štefánika 11, 13, 29, 47, 48
Chata pod Javorinkou 4
Chopok 11, 12, 38, 39, 47

Iľanovo 30
Iľanovské sedlo 31, 33

Jakubčáková 23
Jama 19, 45
Jánska dolina 29, 36
Jasenianska dolina 6
Jasenie 6
Jasná 35, 37, 38, 39
Javorie 29, 34, 36
Jelenská skala 1

Kamenná chata 32
Kaštieľske lazy 26
Kečka 2, 46
Kolesárová 17, 49
Korytnica-kúpele 2
Kosienky 34

Kosodrevina 10, 11, 12
Košarisko 4
Kotliská 7, 47
Kozí chrbát 2, 3, 46
Kozí kameň 23
Krakova hoľa 34
Králička 14, 48
Kráľova hoľa 20, 21, 50
Kráľova skala 20
Krivý most 17
Krížske sedlo 7, 12, 39
Krpáčovo 7, 8, 9
Krúpova hoľa 11, 13, 47
Krúpove sedlo 11, 13, 29, 38
Kufajka 22
Kumštové sedlo 14, 48
Kyslá 3, 6

Latiborská hoľa 46
Lenivá 15
Liptovská Lúžna 44
Liptovská Porúbka 26
Liptovská Teplička 21, 22
Liptovský Ján 26, 27, 28, 29
Lomnistá dolina 6
Lopušná dolina 23
Lučivná 23
Lúčky 34, 36, 37, 38
Ludrová 43
Luková 37, 39

Magura 43
Magurka 42
Machnaté 33, 34
Malužiná 24
Malužinská dolina 24
Malý Salatín 43
Mesiačik 10
Mestská hora 42
Michalovské sedlo 27
Moštenica 3
Mýto pod Ďumbierom 13

Nad Kopcovou 4, 5
Nemecká 5, 24

Nižná Boca 25

Ohnište 27
Ondrejská hoľa 4
Opalisko 30
Orlová 21, 50
Ostré 45
Otupné 35, 38

Pálenica 10
Pálenice 7
Pálenička 7
Panská hoľa 14
Panské sedlo 5
Partizánska Ľupča 40
Pavčina Lehota 31
Pekná vyhliadka 37
Pod Brezinami 9
Pod Krčahovom 34, 36, 37
Pod Oravcovou 17
Pod Orlou skalou 37, 39
Podsuchá 45
Podvrch 16
Pohorelá 19
Pohorelský medokýš 19
Pohronský Bukovec 5
Poľana 12, 35, 39, 47
Poldvorné 22
Polianka 2
Polomka 17
Poludnica 30
Pošova Mlynná 13
Prameň Boženy Němcovej 16
Prameň Sama Chalupku 8, 9
Prameň Zubrovice 50
Prašivá 29
Pred Bystrou 27, 29, 36
Predná Magura 40
Predná Poludnica 30
Predné 24
Predné sedlo 20
Predsuchá 6
Pri Javore 1
Priehyba 18, 49
Priehybka 18, 49

Príslop 10, 12, 39
Púchalky 36
Pusté 33, 34

Rakytovica 30
Ráztocká hoľa 4
Ráztocké lazy 4, 5
Ráztocké sedlo 44
Ráztoka 4, 5
Repiská 35
Rovienky 14, 48
Rovná hoľa 25
Rumanec 40

Salašná 17
Salatín 43, 44
Sedlo Ďurkovej 6, 42, 46, 47
Sedlo pod Babou 2
Sedlo pod Kohútom 43
Sedlo pod Malým Salatínom 43
Sedlo pod Skalkou 46
Sedlo pod Veľkým bokom 24
Sedlo Poľany 12, 35, 38, 39
Sedlo za Lenivou 15, 48
Siná 35
Skala 15
Skalka 7
Slemä 27
Sliačske travertíny 41
Smrekovica 28
Snehová jama 20
Sopotnická dolina 4
Srdiečko 10, 11, 12
Staníkovo 21
Stanišovská dolina 27, 28, 29
Stanišovské sedlo 27, 28
Stará Boca 14, 25
Starobocianska dolina 14
Stredný Sliač 41
Strmý vŕštek 7
Struhárske sedlo 6
Suchá dolina 30
Svarín 24
Svarínska dolina 24
Svidovské sedlo 27

Šachtička 1
Široká dolina 37, 38
Špania Dolina 1
Šumiac 20

Table 23
Tabličky 23
Tajch 4
Tále 9, 10
Telgárt 20, 50
Teplice 45
Trangoška 10, 11, 13
Tri vody 35, 37, 38

Útulňa pod Andrejcovou 19, 49, 50
Útulňa pod Sedlom Ďurkovej 46, 47
Útulňa Ramža 48, 49

Váh 26
Vajskovská dolina 7
Veľká Chochuľa 4, 46
Veľká Riavka 9
Veľká Vápenica 18, 49
Veľký bok 24
Veľký Brankov 45
Veľký Brunov 21
Vikartovce 23
Vrbické pleso 37
Vyšná Boca 14, 15, 25
Vyšné poľany 18
Vyšné sedlo 20
Vyšný Sliač 41
Vyvieranie 31, 33

Zadná hoľa 17, 49
Zámostská hoľa 6, 42, 46
Záturňa 21
Závadka nad Hronom 17
Závažná Poruba 30
Zubová 3
Ždiarska dolina 17
Ždiarska hoľa 7
Ždiarske sedlo 19, 21, 50
Železné 44

Slovník	Słownik	Wörterbuch	Dictionary
brána	brama	Tor	gate
cesta	droga	Weg	road
dolina	dolina	Tal	valley
dom	dom	Haus	house
hora	góra	Berg	mountain
horáreň	leśniczówka	Forsthaus	forester´s house
horská služba	Pogotówie górskie	Bergdienst	mountaineering
hostinec	gospoda	Wirtshaus	inn
hrad	zamek	Burg	castle
hranica	granica	Grenze	border
hrebeň	grań	Grat	comb
chata	schronisko	Hütte	cottage
jaskyňa	jaskinia	Höhle	cave
jazero	jezioro	See	lake
kaplnka	kaplica	Kapelle	chapel
kaštieľ	dwór, kasztel	Schloß	manorhouse
kláštor	klasztor	Kloster	monastery
kostol	kościół	Kirche	church
kotol	kocioł	Kessel	cauldron
kúpalisko	basen, kąpielisko	Schwimmbad	swimming pool
kúpele	uzdrowisko	Bad	spa
lanovka	kolejka linowa	Seilbahn	funicular
les	las	Wald	forest
mesto	miasto	Stadt	town
nábrežie	nabrzeże	Ufer	embankment
námestie	plac, rynek	Platz	square
ostrov	wyspa	Insel	island
pamätník	pomnik	Denkmal	monument
planina	płaskowyż	Ebene	plain
pleso	górskie jezioro	Bergsee	mountain lake
potok	potok	Bach	brook
prameň	źródło	Quelle	spring
priepasť	przepaść	Abgrund	chasm
rázcestie	rozwidlenie	Gabelung	crossroads
reťaz	łancuch	Kette	chain
rieka	rzeka	Fluß	river
roklina	wąwóz	Klamm	ravine
sad	park, sad	Park	orchard
sedlo	przełęcz, siodło	Sattel	mountain saddle
skanzen	skansen	Freilichtmuseum	open-air museum
stena	ściana	Wand	wall
strom	drzewo	Baum	tree
studňa	studnia	Brunnen	well
svah	stok, zbocze	Hang	slope
štít	szczyt	Spitze	peak
teplý prameň	gorące żródło	Thermalbäder	thermal spring
útulňa	chata	Unterstand	shelter
veža	wieża, turnia	Turm	tower
vrch	szyt, góra	Berg	mountain
vrchovina	wyżyna	Bergland	highlands
železnica	kolej	Bahnlinie	railway

Practical information

D – Drevené kostoly (Log churches)
Artikulárny kostol, Svätý Kríž, tel. 044/559 26 22. Opening hours:
June 1- September 30, Mo - Su, 9:00-17:00h, October 1 - May 31, Mo - Su,
9:00-15:00h.

G – Galérie (Galleries)
– **Galéria Petra Michala Bohúňa**, Tranovského 3, Liptovský Mikuláš, tel. 044/552 27 58. Opening hours: Tu - Su, 10:00-17:00h.

H – Horská služba (Mountain Rescue Service)
– **Základná stanica HS: Horská služba Nízke Tatry – sever**, Dom HS, 032 51 Demänovská Dolina, tel. 044/559 16 78
– **Záchranná stanica HS: Horská služba Nízke Tatry – sever**, Chata Opalisko, 032 02 Závažná Poruba, tel. 044/554 71 78
– **Záchranná stanica HS: Horská služba Nízke Tatry – sever**, Chata Čertovica, tel. 044/529 12 45
– **Záchranná stanica HS: Horská služba Nízke Tatry – sever**, Liptovská Teplička, tel. 052/779 81 50
– **Základná stanica HS: Horská služba Nízke Tatry – juh**, Dom HS - Tále, 977 01 Bystrá, tel. 048/617 00 26
– **Záchranná stanica HS: Horská služba Nízke Tatry – juh**, Chata gen. M. R. Štefánika, tel. 048/619 51 20
– **Záchranná stanica HS: Horská služba Nízke Tatry – juh**, Kamenná chata - Chopok, tel. 048/617 00 39
– **Záchranná stanica HS: Horská služba Nízke Tatry – juh**, Kráľova hoľa, tel. 052/773 13 31

CH – Chaty (Cottages)
– **Chata Magurka**, 032 15 Partizánska Ľupča, tel. 044/439 82 79
– **Kamenná chata pod Chopkom**, 977 01 Brezno, tel. 048/617 00 39, e-mail: kamchata@kiwi.sk
– **Chata gen. M. R. Štefánika**, 977 01 Brezno, tel. 048/61 95 120
– **Penzión STIV Čertovica**, 032 34 Malužiná, tel./fax 044/529 14 00 e-mail: certovica@stonline.sk

CH – Chodníky (Paths) (closed from November 1 to June 30)
1. Kotliská – Žiar – yellow mark
2. Poľana – sedlo Siná – yellow mark
3. Dolina Vyvieranie – green mark

I – Informácie (Information)

Information on travel and tourism concerning the region is provided by some bureaux of travel information and promotion in certain areas. Information concerning other regions is provided by the travel agencies.

– **Informačné centrum Mesta Liptovský Mikuláš**, Námestie mieru 1, 031 01 Liptovský Mikuláš, tel. 044/16 186, 552 24 18, fax: 044/551 44 48, e-mail: infolm@trynet.sk, www.lmikulas.sk, www.icm.mikulas.sk
– **Informačné centrum Liptovský Hrádok**, SNP 311, 033 01 Liptovský Hrádok, tel. 044/522 50 60, fax: 044/522 50 59, e-mail: iclh@aprojekt.sk
– **Kultúrne a informačné centrum**, Madačova 3, 034 01 Ružomberok, tel. 044/432 10 96, fax: 044/432 32 16

J – Jaskyne (Caves)

– **Demänovská jaskyňa slobody**, Demänovská Dolina, tel. 044/559 16 73. Opening hours: Tu - Su, January 2 - May 31, September 16 - November 15, December 15 - December 31, 9:00, 11:00, 12:30, 14:00h, June 1 - September 15, 9:00, 10:00, 11:00, 12:00, 13:00, 14:00, 15:00, 16:00h, November 16 - December 14, December 24 - December 26, January 1, closed.
– **Demänovská ľadová jaskyňa**, Demänovská Dolina, tel. 044/554 81 70. Opening hours: Tu - Su, May 15 - May 31, September 1 - September 30, 9:00, 11:00, 12:30, 14:00h, June 1- August 31, 9:00, 10:00, 11:00, 12:00, 13:00, 14:00, 15:00, 16:00h, October 1- May 14, closed.
– **Važecká jaskyňa**, Važec, tel. 044/529 41 71. Opening hours: Tu - Su, May 15 - September 15, 9:00, 10:00, 11:00, 12:00, 13:00, 14:00, 15:00, 16:00h, September 16 - November 30, February 1 - May 14, 10:00, 11:00, 12:30, 14:00h, December 1 - January 31, closed.

N – Národné parky (National parks)

– **Správa NAPANT-u**, Zelená 5, 974 01 Banská Bystrica, tel. 048/413 08 88, 413 08 89
– **Správa NAPANT-u**, SNP 311, Liptovský Hrádok, tel. 044/522 28 75, fax: 044/522 10 82

T – Termálne kúpalisko (Thermal swimming pool)

– **Termálne kúpalisko** Liptovský Ján, tel. 044/520 81 00

Hotel Bystrina
Autocamping Demänovská Dolina

032 51 Demänovská Dolina
Tel. +421 44 / 55 48163-5
e-mail: bystrina@mail.eurotel.sk
www.hotelbystrina.sk

The hotel and car-camping site are located in the attractive environment of the Demänovská valley.

EUROBUILDING a. s.
Chata Björnson

032 51 Demänovská Dolina
Tel. +421 (0)44 / 55 916 77 Fax +421 (0)44 / 55 916 89
e-mail: euro@isternet.sk

Stylish mountain cottages located in the picturesque setting of the Nízke Tatry Mts., only 50 meters from ski tracks.

EUROBUILDING a. s.
Hotel Junior Jasná

032 51 Demänovská Dolina
Tel. +421 (0)44 / 5591571-4 Fax +421 (0)44 / 5591575
e-mail: junior@isternet

The hotel is known for its sporty atmosphere. It stands next to the ski track.

Hotel Lodenica

Nábrežie J. Kráľa 8
033 01 Liptovský Mikuláš
Tel. +421 (0)44/ 5522349, 5520218
Fax +421 (0)44/ 5520217
e-mail: ktklm@isternet.sk
www.isternet.sk/ktklm

The hotel is situated in the pleasant setting on the bank of the Váh River not far away from the city centre.

Hotel TATRIN — Závažná Poruba

032 02 Závažná Poruba
Tel. +421 (0)44 / 5547189
Fax +421 (0)44 / 5547182
e-mail: tatrin@isternet.sk

Accomodation in suites

HOTEL

Stavoindustria L. Mikuláš, a. s.

Ul. 1. mája č. 117, 031 01 LIPTOVSKÝ MIKULÁŠ
Tel. +421 44 / 5522911 recepcia
Tel./ Fax +421 (0)44 / 5522967
e-mail: sekr-si@stavoindustria.sk
www.stavoindustria.sk

Double bedrooms + one bathroom. Cell system of accomodation.

DOM ADRIA

031 01 LIPTOVSKÝ MIKULÁŠ
Bodice 99
Tel./Fax +421 (0)44 / 55 49 335

Accomodation in private houses
Price of breakfast: od 400 do 600 Sk

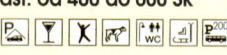

Rekreačná chata
NA REPISKÁCH

Demänovská Dolina – Repiská č. 77
Tel. +421 (0)44/ 5522277 Fax +421 (0)44/ 5514738
e-mail: penzion-fenix@bb.telecom.sk

The cottage is located about 3 km
from the ski centre of Jasná, amidst
quiet spruce forest. It consists
of two independent parts (6/11).

Penzión NON-STOP

Bodice 101
031 01 LIPTOVSKÝ MIKULÁŠ
Tel./Fax +421 (0)44 / 5549205
mobil: 00421 (0)905 / 272 538

An independent struckture at the entry to the Demänovská Dolina valley.

The Town information centre

Námestie mieru 1, 031 01 LIPTOVSKÝ MIKULÁŠ

Tel. +421(0)44/16 186, 552 24 18   Fax +421(0)44/551 44 48
e-mail: infolm@trynet.sk   www.lmikulas.sk   www.icm.mikulas.sk

Free information: accomodation and board facilities of the Liptov region / services / cultural monuments / countryside attractions / cultural and sports events / visit programmes / institutions, enterprises and companies   **Services:** exchange office / accomodation / guide service / translation and interpretation service / the sale of educational-promotion material / fax service / sports activities and organised programme: paragliding, rafting, speleoservice, horse-riding, cycle-tourism with a guide, mountaineering, high-mountain hiking with a mountain guide, ski and snowboarding school, ski-equipment hire service, bicycle hire service, panoramic flights, rafting floating.

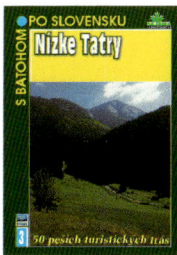
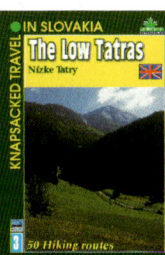
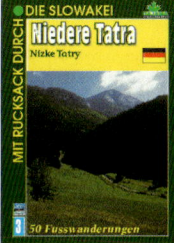
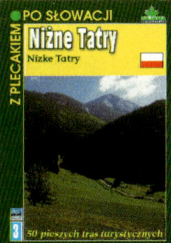

Ľubľanská 2, 831 02 Bratislava
Tel./Fax 02 / 44 631 702
e-mail: geonad@internet.sk   www.dajama.sk

	Rybolov / Fishing / Angeln / Wędkowanie
	Stravovanie / Catering / Verpflegung / Wyżywienie
	Kúpalisko / Swimming pool / Swimmingpool / Basen
	Windsurfing
	Turistika / Hiking / Wandertouristik / Turystyka piesza
	Bežecké lyžovanie / Cross-country ski / Skilanglauf / Narciarstwo biegowe
	Detské hry / Children games / Kinderspiele / Plac zabaw
	Člnkovanie / Boating, rowing / Ruderboote / Łódki, kajaki
	Lyžiarsky vlek / Ski lift / Skilift / Wyciąg narciarski
	Informácie / Information / Informationen / Informacje
	Sauna, solárium / Sauna, solarium / Sauna, Solarium / Sauna, solarium
	Požičovňa športových potrieb / Sport outfit hire service / Sportverleih / Wypożyczalnia sprzętu sportowego
	Hotelové parkovisko – vo dvore / Hotel parking lot, parking on the premises / Hotelparkplatz – Parken im Hof / Parking hotelowy – parkowanie na podwórzu
100	Zmenáreň / Exchange office / Wechselstube / Kantor
	Bufet / Snack bar / Buffet / Bufet
WC	Sociálne zariadenia na izbách / Individual baths / Soziale Einrichtung im Zimmer / Urządzenia sanitarne w pokojach
WC	Spoločné sociálne zariadenia / Common baths / Gemeinsame Badezimmer / Urządzenia sanitarne wspólne
	Kuchyňa / Kitchen / Küche / Kuchnia
	Chladnička / Refrigerator / Kühlschrank / Lodówka
	Tanečná miestnosť / Dancing hall / Tanzsaal / Sala taneczna
	Gril / Grill / Grill / Gril
	Turistický chodník v blízkosti / Hiking path in vicinity / Wanderweg in der Nähe / W pobliżu szlak turystyczny
	Lyžiarska dráha v blízkosti / Ski track in vicinity / Skipiste in der Nähe / W pobliżu narciarska trasa zjazdowa
	Sociálne bezbariérové zariadenia / Barrier-free baths / Behindertengerechte soziale Einrichtung / Urządzenia sanitarne dla niepełnosprawnych
	Minigolf
	Paragliding
	Cykloturistika / Cyclo-tourism / Radwanderungen / Turystyka rowerowa
	Jazda na koni / Horse riding / Reiten / Jazda konna
96	Počet izieb / Number of rooms / Anzahl der Zimmer / Liczba pokoi
	Stolný tenis / Table tennis / Tischtennis / Tenis stołowy
	Volejbal / Volleyball / Volleyball / Siatkówka
TV	Káblová alebo satelitná televízia / Cable or satelite TV / Kabel- oder Satellitenfernseher / Telewizja kablowa lub satelitarna
	Možnosť pobytu s domácimi zvieratami / Possibility of movement with pets / Haustiere erlaubt / Możliwość pobytu ze zwierzętami domowymi
	Konferenčná miestnosť / Conference hall / Konferenzraum / Sala konferencyjna
	Možnosť športových aktivít v okolí, fitnesscentrum / Possibility of sports in environs, fitness centre / Sport- Fitnessaktivitäten in Umgebung möglich / Możliwość zajęć sportowych, fitness
55	Počet miest v reštaurácii / Number of chairs in a restaurant / Anzahl der Plätze in der Gaststätte / Liczba miejsc w restauracji
P 300	Vzdialenosť od autobusovej zastávky / Distance from the bus stop / Entfernung zur Bushaltestelle / Odległość od przystanku autobusowego
	Kaviareň, bar / Café, Bar / Café, Bar / Kawiarnia, Bar
	Biliard / Billiards / Billard / Bilard
R 50	Maximálny počet klientov prijímaných ako skupina v reštaurácii / Maximum number of clients accepted as a group in a restaurant / Maximale Anzahl der Gäste als Gruppe im Restaurant / Maksymalna liczba klientów przyjmowanych jako grupa w restauracji
55	Maximálny počet klientov prijímaných ako skupina / Maximum number of clients accepted as a group / Maximale Anzahl der Gäste als Gruppe / Maksymalna liczba klientów przyjmowanych jako grupa